WHAT IS CONTEXTUAL BIBLE STUDY?

In loving memory of Irene Bristow

What is Contextual Bible Study?

*A practical guide with group studies
for Advent and Lent*

Edited by
John Riches

Contributions by:
Helen Ball
Roy Henderson
Craig Lancaster
Leslie Milton
Maureen Russell

First published in Great Britain in 2010

Society for Promoting Christian Knowledge
36 Causton Street
London SW1P 4ST
www.spckpublishing.co.uk

British Library Cataloguing-in-Publication Data

A catalogue record for this book is available from the British Library

ISBN 978–0–281–06198–3

1 3 5 7 9 10 8 6 4 2

Typeset by Graphicraft Ltd, Hong Kong
Printed in Great Britain by JF Print

Produced on paper from sustainable forests

Contents

————•◦•————

Contents

Part Two
CONTEXTUAL BIBLE STUDIES FOR ADVENT AND LENT

Acknowledgements

More than most books of its type, this volume is the result of many, many people's work, imagination and creativity over some 15 years. To acknowledge the contributions of all those who have supported the development of Contextual Bible Study (CBS) in the UK over this period would be impossible; not to acknowledge at least the contribution of a representative sample would be deeply misleading. So, those who are thanked here must stand for many others. To all, our heartfelt thanks.

Contextual Bible Study has always had strong international roots. First to mention are Gerald West and the members of the Institute for the Study of the Bible at the University of Natal Pietermaritzburg who came to Glasgow to enthuse those who became the original members of the group. Gerald has been back a number of times since and members of the group have visited Pietermaritzburg, drawing insight from the work that continues there.

Among our other international contacts we would mention Pamela Parenzee from the Diocese of Cape Town, who visited us while working in Hemel Hempstead and taught us new aspects of the process, and Hans de Wit of the Free University of Amsterdam, whose project 'Through the Eyes of Another' brought us into a rich fellowship of biblical scholars and practitioners. Our warm thanks, too, to Jonas and Maria Ngomane of the Ecumenical Seminary at Ricatla, who hosted our meetings in Mozambique. Eric Anum, now of the University of Cape Coast in Ghana, spent many years in Glasgow and was a good friend and, in his dissertation, observer and gentle critic of the group.

We were fortunate from the start in having close links with a number of clergy and religious working in the East End of Glasgow. Here we would mention particularly Irene Bristow at St Thomas', Gallowgate; John McLuckie at St John's, Baillieston; Tom Magill at St Dominic's, Craigend; Malcolm Cuthbertson of St George's and St Peter's, Easterhouse; and Sr Gina Cardosi. The freshness and vigour of some of the readings we shared with members of those congregations in the early days gave a special impetus to the work of the group.

Warm thanks are due too to the Scottish Bible Society and to its sometime director, Douglas Campbell, who invited us to collaborate with the Society in its 'Conversations' project. This provided us with valuable resources and the opportunity to engage with a wider section of the Scottish churches and to run training courses across Scotland. Maisie Rendell and Alan Campbell of the Society are enthusiastic supporters and continue to work with us on occasion. It was Douglas who provided us with our most challenging international encounter, the invitation to conduct a Bible study with a visiting delegation of (political) ministers of religion from the People's Republic of China.

We have been most fortunate in the many invitations we have received to work with church groups across Scotland and the UK. We would like to express special thanks to Anne Tomlinson and Susan Macdonald of the Scottish Episcopal Church for their willingness to involve us in their work in equipping all the members of the church for ministry. We should also like to thank those who have worked with CBS in prisons, in particular Jacci Stoyle and Alison Peden.

In the academic world we have had much support. Again, a few names must stand for many. Chris Rowland at Oxford has been a wonderful friend to those who have engaged in more practically orientated readings of the Bible. In Glasgow, John Barclay, Robert Carroll and Alistair Hunter, colleagues in the then Biblical Studies Department, encouraged and supported the research project into African interpretation of the Bible out of which CBS in the UK sprang. Heather Walton has always shown interest and support; a number of students, including Eric Anum and Emmanuel Frimpong from Ghana and the late Happy Mhango from Malawi, have taken up the method and used it in their researches. John Vincent at the Urban Theology Unit in Sheffield has been an enthusiastic supporter. Daniel Patte at Vanderbilt invited us to contribute to the *Global Bible Commentary* and Alison Jack at New College, Edinburgh, similarly invited us to contribute to *The Expository Times*.

CBS has always operated with a small core group whose make-up has constantly changed as people have moved on and been replaced by new members. It is not possible to name here all those who have taken part, but in addition to those responsible for the present volume, and those already mentioned, a few others must be named. Stephen Smyth introduced us to some of the working of group dynamics and helped us to tighten up the process. He also worked together with the Bible Society in developing the 'Conversations' programme and the *Companion* that we produced together. Susan Millar took over at the Bible Society where Stephen left off and gave much support to the group. Hugh Foy has been an enthusiastic supporter, both as an active member of the group and subsequently, and is always on the lookout for opportunities to use CBS. Russell Jones, formerly of St Bride's, Hyndland, built up one of the most active congregational CBS groups after one residential conference before becoming a member of the 'core' group. Robert Hill and Karen Wenell were long-time members of the group who, like so many others, have made sustained contributions on which this volume depends. Andrew Scott was a most insight-ful observer and recorder of the Lenten sessions at St Bride's, Hyndland.

Finally, our thanks to all who have participated in reading the Bible with us. It is their readings which inform this book and which we hope will inspire others to emulate what they have done.

Introduction

———•◆•———

This book is designed as a practical guide to Contextual Bible Study, a prayerful way of reading the Bible which allows a group of people to explore the text together by means of close and careful reading. Within its pages you will find a description of the method and its development in the UK, some practical guidelines for running a series of sessions and a set of questions for Advent and Lent for all three years, A, B, C, of the Common Lectionary. There is also an account of one such set of discussions developed in an ecumenical group in the West End of Glasgow. You will not find reports of amazing moments of illumination, of dramatic, life-changing choices; but there is a record of a steady growth of insight into the text, a growing understanding of the place of Jesus both in the Gospel story and in the lives of believers.

As we have worked with CBS over the last 15 years, we have been constantly struck by the positive way in which people have reacted to this method of reading the Bible. People who have not read the Bible much, who are often quite worried about whether they are properly qualified or equipped to read it at all, find that they have gifts and skills to bring to the texts which can make a real contribution to the group's understanding.

When we embarked on this exploration of CBS, one of our group, Leslie Milton, undertook a survey of methods of Bible study in the West of Scotland. Typically, there were two such methods. First, many people would allow themselves to be guided in their reading by William Barclay's *Daily Study Bible*.

This was a liberal evangelical reading of the Bible (how liberal, many of his readers did not appreciate), full of lively anecdote and historical detail, which made a direct connection between the stories and debates in the New Testament texts and the personal experience of the reader. Second, in more conservative evangelical churches, the weekday Bible study would be led by the minister who would give an extended exposition of the text to be followed by questions for clarification. Such studies would presume an agreed doctrinal framework and would in a measure be informed by historical knowledge of the setting and circumstances of the text. They were, above all, teaching opportunities for the minister.

The excitement of CBS lies in its ability to unlock 'ordinary' readers' abilities and skills and to draw out their insights into the text. Through conversation arising from the text, people can share their understanding and explore the way the text helps them make sense of their lives.

A lot depends on the facilitators' ability to ensure that people in the group listen to and respect each other, have space to express their views without attempting to dominate others, and are encouraged to share their insights. In the best sessions, there is a quality of conversation, of discourse, which can be empowering and liberating. Asked what they valued about the process, one congregation in Glasgow's East End said it was the fact that they could have a real conversation with each other, quite different from the kind of talk – the 'tinny rattle' – that they might meet in the pub and the betting shops. In our experience, CBS creates a space where this kind of discourse can occur; it is deeply needed in a church where we often seem to have lost the ability to discuss matters theologically.

What kind of understanding of the Bible does CBS imply? What understanding of it does a person need to have, in order to take part in such discussions? We would see CBS as a pragmatic way of approaching the Bible. People should come to the study willing to listen to the text and to each other, and ready to contribute as they feel able. They may come with strong expectations, based on past experience of Bible reading; they may simply come with an open mind, willing to recognize wisdom and insight where it occurs, willing to engage in dialogue and to critique as appropriate. We choose to read the Bible because it is the Church's book, and because it is our experience that it can bring insight and liberation, personal and communal transformation.

CBS is above all something that is learnt and enjoyed in the doing of it. However much one talks about it, there is no substitute for actually meeting with a group of people and engaging in discussion around a passage of Scripture. To give a taste of what can happen when one participates in the CBS process, we have included in 'boxes' throughout the book a series of illustrative examples, as well as a more detailed account of one series of studies. And in order to encourage readers to translate theory into practice, in Part Two of the book we offer a series of CBS questions for the lectionary readings in Advent and Lent.

Part One

A LIFE-CHANGING APPROACH TO GROUP BIBLE STUDY

1

CBS: What is it? Where did it come from?

The name Contextual Bible Study (CBS) may not be familiar. It is a way of reading the Bible in groups, which over the last 50 or so years has spread across the world from Latin America to South Africa and from there to various parts of Europe, including the UK. Our group in the West of Scotland has been working with it and finding it fruitful for the last 15 years. As we use it, CBS is a prayerful way of reading the Bible in a group, which allows the group to explore the text together, to read it closely and carefully, and where appropriate to explore its literary and historical context. And having done that, it enables the people in the group to shed light on their lives and their contexts – personal, local, familial, national and international.

As its name suggests, CBS is a method that encourages readers to read the Bible in ways appropriate to their own contexts and which allow them to engage in dialogue with one another to address current concerns in the light of the biblical texts. Typically, it will be facilitated, rather than led, by someone who will guide the group through a series of questions which help them read the text closely and in ways which enable them to hear the different voices contained in it, and to discern the resonance between their own context and the text itself.

This may (or may not) then lead to the group formulating some plan of action arising out of their discussions. Or it may lead to a widening of people's horizons, experience and understanding. The questions put to the text play an important role in the process. They are designed to be open questions, encouraging people to explore the text and their own reactions to it. Above all, it is a method which encourages participants to engage in open dialogue with each other in the light of Scripture.

From South Africa to Scotland

Contextual Bible Study in Scotland began as a scholarly exchange. In 1995 Professor Gerald West of the University of Natal visited the Faculty of Divinity at Glasgow University. At a packed public lecture, he explained the CBS methodology pioneered at the Institute for the Study of the Bible (ISB) in Pietermaritzburg, a process whereby, during the apartheid era, socially engaged biblical scholars read the Bible with groups of very poor and marginalized people. Meetings held in segregated townships gave people courage to oppose the harsh conditions under which they lived, sometimes leading them to formulate and carry out often costly programmes of action. West was a missionary for the movement; he urged upon his hearers that it would be equally feasible to use his methods in other contexts.

After the lecture, those present – biblical scholars, theological students, ordained and lay church leaders – began to explore what it would mean to use CBS locally. Where might they find groups of poor, marginalized people in the West of Scotland? And was it possible to read the Bible with such people, with the kind of transformational effect that West described? Might such ways of reading the Bible encourage community activism, enable people in Glasgow's East End and peripheral housing estates to bring change to their communities?

4

The CBS Group, formed shortly thereafter, was an ecumenical group made up of members of the Department of Biblical Studies at the University of Glasgow and clergy and lay members from across the churches in Glasgow, most of whom had received formal training in reading the Bible. The group set about its new mission with commendable dedication; some months were spent practising the CBS method and thinking about who the 'poor' and 'marginalized' might be in the Scottish context. Clearly the poor were the economic poor, whose paucity of material resources restricted their opportunities regarding education, employment or housing. Among the marginalized were the disabled, prisoners and former prisoners, women, gay and lesbian people, ethnic minorities.[1] However, although CBS was ready for its debut, there was a peculiar complication. The South Africans had resolved to work only with organized groups of poor and marginalized people, those who were active in the fierce political struggle of the apartheid era. Finding similar groups in the West of Scotland who would be interested in Bible study was more difficult.

In the CBS process, context is seminal. Concerted groups of poor people, 'the organized poor', were easily identifiable in the black townships of apartheid South Africa. Moreover, the Bible enjoyed wide respect and authority among all sections of South African society – black, white, liberal and nationalist – and was used freely in debates on both sides of the political conflict. The Bible had a particularly precious meaning to the poor in this context: Eric Anum, a Ghanaian Presbyterian minister who studied at Glasgow University, described the Bible as 'an icon of their hope for life'.[2]

By contrast, in the West of Scotland, CBS found organized groups committed to working with the poor and marginalized – for example, charities working with the homeless or ex-offenders – but not 'the organized poor' *per se*. Moreover, far from enjoying wide respect, by the end of the twentieth century the Bible had lost its place in Scottish life. In 1997 the historian Callum Brown observed, 'In extremely large numbers, the people have stopped going to church, stopped becoming church members, and no longer recognise a substantive religious influence in their social lives.'[3] Thus for many poor, marginalized people in this context, reading the Bible was counter-cultural and unnatural. Whereas in South Africa Gerald West found the Bible such a pervasive text in the lives of most people that it could easily be deployed as a resource to help the poor, this was not at all the case in the West of Scotland.[4]

Development in Scotland

Although it proved difficult to locate and read with 'the organized poor', the CBS team in Scotland began reading the Bible with a number of groups, often church groups, committed to helping disadvantaged people, as well as with churches in the East End of Glasgow. One of the first studies the team undertook was with an ecumenical study group in the city's inner East End, where it was agreed to read some of the psalms of exile. As is described in more detail later in this chapter, these chimed in with the situation of the churches in an area that had seen rapid social change and the breakdown of former communities. In Hamilton, Lanarkshire, an ecumenical group working with the homeless met to study Psalm 94. Verse 20, 'Can rulers be allied with you, who frame mischief by statute?' prompted a discussion about recent legislation on housing benefit. When members of a church housing initiative, a housing association, a centre for the unemployed and local churches met with CBS facilitators to read James 2.14–17, the conversation centred upon ways of assisting unemployed and homeless people in Clyde-bank.

During this initial phase, the CBS group was still exploring and experimenting with the methodology of CBS. A group member recalls, 'We were in one sense learning to unlearn a lot of what we brought with us from historical critical studies of the Bible.'

Gerald West, in common with others, had distinguished different ways of reading a text: reading to distinguish its historical content and meaning; focusing on the text itself, its narrative, argument, ideas and metaphors; and reading it in the light of certain shared concerns and questions. (These ways of reading are explored in more detail in Chapter 3.) For those schooled in historical criticism, the temptation was to delve into the reality behind the text and to get so caught up in that enquiry that there was never time to ask what its relevance might be to the present context. In consequence, the CBS Group soon found itself focusing very much on 'reading the text', exploring the stories of the Old Testament and the Gospels as stories, and savouring the rich poetry of the Psalms.

The group was beginning to focus on 'reading *with*' others: entering into conversations with different groups, learning to see and hear the texts afresh as they were reflected through other people's experiences. The early CBS experience of reading the Bible with groups active in working with disadvantaged people proved that such encounters could lead to lively discussions. Socially concerned biblical scholars and socially active groups had plenty to say about Bible texts on themes of social justice. Such sessions offered the participants mutual encouragement and reinforcement.

There were times when this led to a genuine exchange of views: a conversation could open up new perspectives and help

CBS outside a submarine base

In November 2006, as part of the year of protest at the gates of the Faslane Trident submarine base, a small ecumenical group of seven protesters shared a CBS session based on Luke 12.49–53, 'Jesus the cause of division'. It was a beautiful, crisp, early winter's morning. Few of us had ever met before. We stood near the gate, beside the security fence and razor wire, with guard dogs barking occasionally in the distance – and nuclear weapons lurking probably nearer.

After hearing the different initial reactions to the passage, we named the tensions that we could find within it. This led to a discussion about how Jesus might have understood tensions that he and his followers faced, the opposition which they encountered from people in positions of power in their society. Only then did we begin to explore the tensions experienced by Christians today, specifically by Christians opposed to Trident.

The final question asked what each individual would take away from the experience. The overriding impression was of the incongruity of sharing Scripture so richly with a group of strangers in such a beautiful landscape but in the shadow of nuclear destruction. Maybe this was not incongruous at all.

members of the group see themselves and their lives in new and transformative ways. One such early experience, that of a group working with prisoners and ex-offenders, is described below. Resonance between the early church's grappling with racial and social diversity in Galatians 3, and its overcoming of those forces 'in Christ', could speak at a very deep level to people caught in similarly destructive divisions in Glasgow's still heavily sectarian East End.

Yet at other times the conversation failed to rise to the level of real dialogue. The readers and the groups had pre-formed views and the discussions moved along predictable lines. Some of the participants in these early sessions mentioned that they felt that the CBS facilitators had a 'hidden agenda' and 'imposed their views and questions on them'.[5] Essentially, therefore, such sessions were closed readings of the Bible. And a closed system is ultimately unfulfilling. The CBS method, it was becoming clear, was not a fail-safe approach, but one which required constant thought and reflection on the part of all, and in particular of facilitators, if true dialogue was to emerge.

This is a continuing question for any discussion group, whether centred on the Bible or not. How do such groups become occasions of real exchange and illumination and not merely opportunities for their leaders to impart their views to others? It was an issue with which the CBS group wrestled from the beginning. Were the questions put to the readers genuinely open? Or did the leaders know beforehand what kinds of answers were expected? Did the fact that the facilitators had chosen the passage and the questions prejudice the chances of real dialogue emerging from the discussions?

In order for CBS to be genuinely open, there must be multiple readings and multiple answers. The group realized that in order to empower the process, it was necessary to sacrifice some control and direction. The sessions needed various entry and exit points, allowing people to approach the text from all kinds of contexts and permitting all kinds of answers. There had to be the capacity for the unexpected, for the Holy Spirit to work through Scripture in ways that none of the participants could have anticipated.

There were other, more pragmatic considerations which also gave the group cause for thought. We were by now receiving

9

invitations to conduct sessions with an increasingly wide range of groups in Scotland and the UK. Such invitations came not only from groups working in urban priority areas but also from middle-class church people who no longer felt confident in their ability to read the Bible. If at first we had wanted to concentrate on reading with the poor and marginalized, now the invitation was to enlarge ways of expressing the faith, seeking a new theological language in which to do so. Invitations to work with such churches were not ones we could turn down. In order to meet such requests, however, we needed to enlarge the group of people who were trained to run CBS sessions. That meant including people who were not necessarily professional theologians or biblical scholars.

A pot-luck supper with student Christians

In November 2009, we responded to a request from a couple of students in a Scottish university. They were trying to re-establish the Student Christian Movement and this was to be their first meeting: a vegetarian pot-luck followed by a CBS session. They had chosen the theme 'Life to the Full'; the passage selected was John 10.7–16. Seven students came along. Most of them knew one or both of the organizers, but not each other.

The session took a little time to get under way: partly to allow us to finish off the food and partly to begin to jell as a group. We explored the different characters and groups present in and around the text. Then, having identified a number of other possible themes, we reflected on what 'life to the full' might mean: both in the passage and, crucially, as a young person trying to live as a Christian in a university setting today. This developed into a very honest and searching conversation – with a lot of laughter.

After the session the students headed off to the pub. There was no doubt that the group enjoyed the whole experience of sharing together – including sharing the Scriptures. Their key feedback: it was good to have a Bible study session which did not 'try to tell you all the answers'.

Training for CBS

Running a Bible study session that is genuinely open is much more difficult than running a discussion for like-minded people in a single-issue group. The training courses that we ran for facilitators proved an excellent opportunity for us all to reflect on these questions. Here we could discuss with participants how to choose questions that were genuinely open, and how to agree with study groups what texts to read. We could consider what skills and competencies to look for in the readers in a group; and reflect on the role of facilitators in enabling dialogue. We were fortunate in being joined at this point by Brother Stephen Smyth, who had a wealth of experience in teaching drama. With his help, the group developed a greater understanding of the dynamics of managing groups: how to organize the seating, use visual aids, work with different sizes of groups; and how to plan the timing of the questions, so that meetings could finish punctually. We also adopted the practice of offering groups a choice of Scripture passages at the beginning of a session.

By tightening the structure, putting the process itself at the centre, the CBS group opened up CBS, both intellectually and spiritually. The group collaborated with the Scottish Bible Society, running a nationwide training programme in the CBS methodology, and producing a handbook, *Conversations*, to assist facilitators. Courses were run in Ayr, Edinburgh, Glasgow, Perth, the Scottish Borders and Newcastle. The Scottish Bible

Society held a bank of Contextual Bible Studies on their website, for public use. These initiatives were enthusiastically received.

The group ran popular taster sessions, designed to introduce new people to the method and allow them to see if they wanted to sign up for the course. Fifty people came along to one of the very first sessions, including participants from all the main denominations, from the Iona Community and from independent evangelical churches. Ezra 3 was the text chosen for the evening; there was a free and open discussion with different views coming from all over the hall, and with no sense of people standing on denominational or doctrinal positions. One participant commented after the session that the use of two facilitators who would discourse (and disagree) with each other modelled a new form of leadership. This use of two facilitators had gradually emerged as a practice that we felt comfortable with as a group and which was now being recognized as reflecting the values and aims of this kind of Bible study.

The CBS Group was now committed to training people as facilitators who had fewer connections to academic study of the Bible than those who had formed the initial group, and who would be able to represent a much wider variety of aims. As the number of people involved grew, with recruits coming largely from churches with middle-class constituencies and individualistic traditions, the group's original emphasis upon social transformation shifted towards individual growth and transformation. In our work with local churches, an introductory session or short series of CBS, together with training for new facilitators, has empowered church groups to run their own studies as often as they like, in their own environment. The professional theologians committed to the group are mediators to the wider world of this flexible, locally responsive CBS.

At the same time, the expansion of the project has allowed the CBS group to explore social transformation as it engages with different groups in uniquely different circumstances. For example, in our work among prisoners and ex-prisoners in the central belt of Scotland, facilitators have built up relationships carefully over time, using CBS to bring something of the Gospel message to some of the most disparaged and vulnerable people in society.

Reading the Bible with prisoners

During the past 15 years, the group has been involved in three prison projects, reading the Bible with ex-offenders in Glasgow, in a women's prison in Stirling and in a Scottish men's prison. The Hopeful Men's Group, with whom we worked in the mid-1990s, were men involved with the prisoners' charity Hope, in the East End of Glasgow, addressing the culture of violence that shapes young men as they grow up. CBS readers and the Hopeful Men's Group read Scripture together, discussing ideals of maleness that did not involve physical violence. Ephesians 5.21–33 drew a strong response from the group, who thought that the text gave men too much power over their wives, but also that it made unreasonable demands on men. It felt to the members of the group as though society, the Church, made impossibly high demands of their family life; anxiety and frustration broke out in acts of violence when, inevitably, wives and children did not live up to such expectations. A discussion about Galatians 3.23–29 considered stereotypes and divisions encountered by members of the group in their everyday lives. Released from prison just a day earlier, one young man could barely stop talking about the divisions he experienced in his world – tensions between Catholics and Protestants, being separated from his family in prison, the stigma of being marked out by society as a jailbird. At the end of the evening, a member of the group, a Marist brother, remarked, 'I doubt if that young man has ever talked so freely about himself as tonight.'

At Cornton Vale Women's Prison, Stirling, chaplain Alison Peden began weekly Contextual Bible Studies in 2001. This project has been of considerable academic interest, and is discussed by Louise Lawrence in her recently published book, *The Word in Place*, and by Peden herself in her 2005 article in *The Expository Times.*[6] Peden describes how eagerly the women responded to the passages and made connections between their own lives and the Bible narrative: 'The women were right there with Jesus in Gethsemane – they had felt and recognised his abandonment in their own experience.'[7] She modified the CBS process, moulding it to suit the particular needs of the group. She facilitated alone, because it had taken her some time to win the women's trust, and she decided not to write up the group's contributions: 'In prison, there is considerable anxiety about having things written down – a fear that they might somehow become evidence about a prisoner.' Working in a plenary group, rather than in small groups, made it easier for the facilitator to manage the occasionally volatile emotional dynamics of the sessions and helped the women to stay focused on reading the Bible together.[8]

In 2005 the CBS group were invited to work with male prisoners as part of a project of the prison learning centre, helping the prisoners develop dialogue, listening and reflecting skills. In prison, there are few opportunities for small groups to sit quietly, talk freely about themselves and reflect on their lives. The CBS process is open-minded and inclusive; in a noisy, stressful place, the CBS sessions were places of calm and mutual respect. During the first session, the group read 'The Guid Samaritan' from Jamie Stewart's *The Glasgow Gospel*; the men enjoyed the Glasgow dialect and the humour in the passage and were able to offer new insights from this familiar story. Over the following three years, regular meetings were held with small groups of prisoners, some with a church background and others with none. The passages read were usually Gospel stories and parables; sometimes the men chose a passage themselves.

The CBS group's prison work has now ended, although it may be resumed whenever fresh opportunities present themselves. The sessions are remembered by the facilitators who participated in them as inspiring, and as glimpses of God's power. They felt humbled by the openness of those who responded: 'There were occasions when we felt we were treading on sacred ground,' recalled a CBS facilitator, 'when the Bible passage connected with someone in a deeply moving and personal way.'

Finding God's love in prison

One CBS facilitated in prison was the story of Jesus cleansing the Temple (Matthew 21.12). The men explored the themes of violence and authority. They saw a contrast between Jesus' actions, standing up for the downtrodden, and society where money and status matter and bullies get results. They said that in their experience, showing the emotion of caring could be a sign of weakness. One man, who had a history of violence, told the story of a time when he had been segregated. Someone, probably a prison warden, put a chocolate bar under his cell door. To him this was a gesture far more powerful than hostility or aggression. It is often hard for prisoners to accept others' generosity and be open to the love of God. However, one or two men said that sharing the Bible story together reminded them of God's goodness in the past and the surprising places to find it in the present.

Reading the Bible with churches

But most of the groups expressing an interest in CBS have been churches. The CBS group has made an enduring commitment to reading the Bible with them. The churches occupy a sadly reduced status in Scottish society; across the denominational spectrum congregations have been dwindling, collection plates emptying, churches closing, clergy and laity alike feeling demoralized and worried about the future. In many ways they are indeed among the marginalized.

Early in its ministry, the CBS group met with an ecumenical Lent group in the East End of Glasgow. This was an area where large tracts of land had been cleared of housing, with a consequent massive drop in population. The churches, which 40 years before had been influential, at the centre of vigorous communities, now found themselves sidelined and powerless, in a community struggling with drug abuse and random violence. Reading psalms of exile together, these church people responded to the pain of the ancient poems. Their exile was in their own part of the city, where they had grown up and raised their families; their sorrow was that their children would not come to church with them any more, and their grandchildren would not go to Sunday school. Yet these readings were not only about loss and exile; the psalms also struck deep chords with those who despite their loss were keeping their church communities alive and doing their best to tackle the deep social problems in their area.

The CBS approach to reading the Bible has proved exceptionally valuable to the churches. First, the process demands that congregations eventually move beyond grieving for the past and complaining about the present, towards renewal and rebuilding, a more constructive future together. Second, CBS helps people to recover their ability to read the Bible. That Christian people would not be Bible readers may seem a contradiction in terms. However, some Catholic and Anglo-Catholic churches have very little tradition of Bible reading; some Protestant churches prize the Bible highly, yet Bible reading and exposition are reserved for ordained 'experts', inhibiting people in the pews. The CBS method of reading the text in a group was new to many, and people experienced it as empowering. They were amazed to discover how much they, as a group, could find in a passage of Scripture. There was a feeling of excitement and energy about these sessions. Some said that this was what they understood by the Holy Spirit being at work in the Church.

CBS within the churches developed as a lively grassroots movement. The Bible was no longer the preserve of trained biblical scholars; across Scotland, groups of Christians of all denominations were reading Scripture together in their own context, listening for God's word and being challenged and transformed by it. Yet the CBS group has also been invited to lead Bible studies with the church hierarchy. The religious leaders of the cities of Belfast, Liverpool and Glasgow meet every three years in Glasgow, a custom going back to the time of the troubles in Northern Ireland. On two occasions, the CBS group was asked to run sessions for these leaders. During the studies the leaders discussed the future of the three cities; in particular, their religious divisions, the waning influence of the churches, and their sense of place as cities built beside rivers.

Church leaders have recognized the missional potential of the CBS process. In 2004, the Scottish Episcopal Church asked for a series of studies for their Provincial Conference, a remark-able gathering at which around 300 clergy and lay people from all over Scotland came together in fellowship to renew their faith, taking as their theme the story of the Feeding of the Five Thousand. A group of facilitators were trained in CBS methods for the conference. Since then, the Scottish Episcopal Church has embraced CBS with real enthusiasm. CBS is offered among the Church's resources for vestries and small churches. It is used as part of the process for mission discernment, on clergy refresher days and congregational retreats, and sometimes for conflict resolution. Many of the more than 50 facilitators who were trained for the conference continue to play their part in helping their communities to develop. Some of the stories told throughout this book will illustrate the remarkably creative forms of church life that have sprung from the subsequent work of these facilitators in their home communities.

CBS – Scottish and global

While being rooted in its locality, the Scottish CBS movement is also part of an international exchange complex of readers reflecting upon and sharing their experiences with other groups that are reading the Bible contextually together. This is important for a number of reasons. First, our engagement with the international network of academic readers of the Bible challenges CBS and keeps it intellectually fresh and involved. Second, groups are affirmed and encouraged by being invited to take part in academic projects. Members of the CBS group at St Bride's Church, Hyndland, for example, were delighted to see some of their readings in print in *The Expository Times*.[9] Finally, CBS is thereby lifted out of the purely local and placed in a global context: a much wider network of groups reading the Bible in a variety of different cultures.

One such intercultural exchange took place in Mozambique in 2000. It was organized by Leslie Milton, who had attended the original meeting with Gerald West in Glasgow in 1995 and was now teaching at the Ecumenical Seminary in Ricatla. The CBS group met for Bible study with a Mozambican group and together read the Old Testament story in Ezra 3 of the

CBS with Chinese government officials

We read the Bible with a group of ministers of religious affairs from the People's Republic of China. They were on a visit to the UK to discover how the British government dealt with the presence of religious bodies within their country. We chose the short passage about Jesus' true family from Mark 3.31–35, which produced a series of lively discussions. Asked what struck them about the passage, the Chinese deputy minister of religion replied that it reminded her of a passage in Confucius. However, they had questions for us: if a member of a Buddhist family becomes a Christian, how does he regard his physical brothers and sisters? We talked together about the generous and inclusive scope of 'Whoever does the will of God is my brother and sister and mother.'

laying of the foundation stone of the Temple. The people of Mozambique were still living in the aftermath of a terrible civil war; the group shared the mixed emotions of the Jewish people gathered for the ceremony, the great shouts of joy indistinguishable from the sound of people weeping. As they recounted their experiences of the war, they also expressed their resolute determination to rebuild their country.

CBS took part in an international project undertaken by the Free University of Amsterdam and the Netherlands Reformed Church. In 2000 Professor Hans de Wit proposed an 'Intercultural Reading of the Bible': groups from all over the world were invited to read the same passage, the story of the Samaritan woman at the well, and then to share their reading with another group on a different continent.[10] The CBS group was twinned with a group in Ghana and read the passage with members of St Dominic's Roman Catholic Church in the East End of Glasgow. In their discussions, the Scottish group focused on the life-changing conversations between Jesus and the Samaritan woman. Asked for examples of similar conversations in their own lives, a Catholic man described the help he had received from a member of the Orange Lodge when he had been in trouble. This Orangeman had been there for him, day and night: 'He was,' he said, 'the embodiment of Christianity, the epitome of kindness. He opened my eyes, which had been closed by instruction.' This was different from the reading of the group in Ghana: they had particularly noticed the way the woman told her friends and neighbours about Jesus and this led them to think of the story as a challenge to go out and preach to their colleagues at work.

Island retreat

The setting was a silent retreat on an island, for clergy and their partners; the passage that of the encounter between the unnamed woman at the well and Jesus (John 4), read across the four days of the gathering. Late on the first evening the group pictured the opening scene of the story where Jesus sits down by a well, tired, hot and thirsty. What jumped out for the assembled group in their own tiredness after a long journey was Jesus' ability to ask another – a surprising other – for help; to express his human needs. Several of those present remarked that their training had conditioned them into suppressing such vulnerability, to be the giver, never the receiver. What would it feel like to ask for help in the way Jesus did? This theme was revisited several times in the next few days and during the retreat people grew in their readiness to express their fears and needs to others.

CBS readings by Scottish groups also contributed to the *Global Bible Commentary*, conceived and edited by Daniel Patte at Vanderbilt University. Invited to produce a reading of

Ephesians from a Scottish perspective, a number of groups came together in partnership for this undertaking; they recorded their readings, sent them in and then attended a final day conference. The results of this collaboration are to be found in a chapter on Ephesians in the *Global Bible Commentary*.[11]

The quality of discourse both distinguishes and links together the many readings the CBS group has conducted over the past 15 years. The best language with which to explore our understanding of God is our own language, and the CBS method of reading equips people with a language with which to reflect both theologically and authentically. The method encourages people to pick up and make their own the images and narrative fragments of Scripture, the telling phrases which can help them to make sense of their own shifting experience. The CBS process offers the structure whereby these observed images and fragments can become the building blocks of a new theological language for the use of all those who take the time to reflect together in conversation. Identifying and nurturing these opportunities is the purpose of the CBS group.

Summary

The Scottish CBS group began as a small gathering of academics and trained readers fired by stories of the way that reading the Bible could empower groups in the poorest and most disadvantaged sections of South African society. As they sought to emulate the work of CBS in the very different context of Scotland in the 1990s they began to put rather different constructions on the meaning of 'poor and marginalized'. This in turn meant looking for different patterns of social transformation, working with many different kinds of groups who seek to address the social and communal needs of a complex post-industrial society.

Alongside this came a growing awareness that this way of reading the Bible answered a deep need within the churches themselves and their members. People who had lost confidence in their ability to read the Bible discovered that they could draw unexpected strength from it and recover the ability to talk and think theologically together. In this way CBS has developed into an inclusive movement, open to all kinds of readers in many different situations. It is the story of the power of Scripture, mediated through a uniquely enabling process, working to transform people's lives, individually and communally, in ways they could never have imagined.

2

CBS: What will it do?

It has been said that the use of CBS is 'fresh and transforming'. It is fresh because it dismantles the distinction between 'qualified' readers, people who have studied the Bible in depth and who have a vast knowledge of its history and traditions, and 'unqualified' readers, who must sit at the feet of those who have 'the knowledge'. And it is 'transforming' in that it develops skills of listening and valuing the contribution of all the members of a group, who often find that the discussion challenges them to think of issues in ways that call into question conventional ways of thinking. It allows people to engage in 'significant discourse', to come to terms with the way in which they have changed or are being challenged to change.

A CBS conversation includes within it talk about God, and the way in which the historical authors spoke about God in their own situation. It explores the way in which God is spoken of between the participants in their current situation. In this chapter we shall look at some of the ways in which these aspects of CBS can be seen to operate.

CBS and locality

Contextual Bible Study is in an important sense 'local'. When you join a CBS group, you will almost certainly be joining with people who come from your own area, or who have some shared experience. CBS groups are set up to help people discuss the issues that are closest to home, whether those are the things that are happening in their daily lives, or important things that are going on in the community that surrounds them. One of the most common experiences in CBS is a deepening of friendship and understanding among a small group of people. Gathered around the Bible, they find that they are able to discuss issues that are important to them, which the normal round of small talk does not readily include.

As we saw in the previous chapter, CBS first came to Britain through conversations with Christians in other parts of the world who had developed a way of reading the Bible that helped people understand more fully the circumstances of their lives. Often this work was being done in places where there were very clear issues in the surrounding society, with which the participants wanted to engage more fully. Groups like these continue to meet throughout the world. Thus a CBS group is more than something that takes place in a local church hall or someone's living room. CBS connects people across the world, living in very different circumstances but united in a simple belief that the Bible can provide a word for them as they try to engage in the complexity of their lives. Let us now consider two situations where CBS has enabled people to relate biblical texts to their contemporary lives.

Stories of hope: a Brazilian experience

One of the earliest experiences of CBS was in Brazil, in a group known as the Centre for Biblical Studies. This group continues to gather people together for workshops and training sessions, focusing on how to draw relationships and lines of connection between what is found in biblical stories and the situation in contemporary Brazil. The workshops bring together people who lead or participate in Bible study groups both in the major cities and in rural communities. The social and political issues that are to the fore in the lives of these communities often find deep resonances with the stories of the Old Testament.

In particular, Bible studies are done among people who have been removed from the land on which they have traditionally lived, those known in Portuguese as *sem terra*, or 'landless people'. Many Old Testament stories come to mind in such a context, such as the promise to Abraham of a plentiful land that would provide for the needs of all his descendants, or the time of slavery in Egypt when the people dreamed of freedom, the Exodus narrative, and God's leading of the people to their own land. All these are inspirational stories for people who feel that they have been removed from lands that they count as their own.

Such stories can take an unexpected turn when heard by people who relate them to their own circumstances. For example, one group leader described how the organizers set up studies with landless people on the plague narratives of Exodus, in the expectation that the people would identify with the Israelites, and cast the ruling landowner class in Brazil as Pharaoh and the Egyptians. In one such study, the participants concluded that they were more like the plague of frogs, the ones who would pester and cause annoyance until their freedom was won. The leaders of the group were not only surprised by this image, but also felt that they had learned something important regarding the fresh and transforming nature of CBS. The studies should not start with a set of outcomes, of things that people are expected to learn or 'get', but should rather enable people to engage with the text and understand their own lives in new ways. This may allow people to appreciate more deeply how God is active in the life of their community. The reading of the Bible is thus a focus of hope and an encouragement to action.

Lives changed: personal transformation and action in the community

At a meeting of people interested in Contextual Bible Study held in 2005 at a retreat in the hills above São Paulo, the participants shared a number of reasons for being engaged in CBS. One older man had trained for the priesthood while still young. He had become disillusioned with the institution of the Roman Catholic Church, and had distanced himself from Christianity for many years. He found the Church controlling, and too much concerned with its own self-preservation and the propagation of dogmas that did not relate directly to the lives of ordinary people. He had discovered a new connection with his faith through Bible study. He was no longer interested in being part of the Church, but had found freedom through CBS meetings to explore God in relation to his own life.

One woman present was an active member of her Roman Catholic parish, but had found no place for her sense of vocation within the male hierarchy. Her involvement with CBS had given her an opening into work with young offenders in São Paulo, and through this she had become a chaplain in the prison. With little formal education she had found a vocation and a place in her church community which would traditionally have been denied her. Her local priest, who had initially been unsupportive and obstructed her interest in reading the Bible, had become increasingly appreciative of her gifts, and now encouraged her involvement in the life of the local parish, where she was a Bible study leader and took part in the Sunday services.

Another woman was involved in a national organization that encouraged participation in democracy, particularly in rural communities. Through the work of CBS she brought her own Christian commitment to her work in impoverished communities. Working largely with women in communities where traditionally they were expected to be involved only in domestic life, she developed Bible studies that were aimed at increasing political involvement at a local level, particularly in preparing people to be monitors in local and national elections. Through the meetings of the groups she facilitated, the participants, many of whom were illiterate, and who engaged with Bible stories by hearing them or through pictorial representations, became more confident in expressing themselves, in analysing situations, and in community leadership.

Stories of hope: a South African experience

CBS in South Africa has placed a similar emphasis on helping people understand their political and economic situation more fully. In 2003 the Ecumenical Service for Social and Economic Transformation (ESSET), an organization under the direction of the South African Council of Churches, ran a series of Bible studies in rural communities across the country. Groups of people in rural areas, one in the north of the country and two in different parts of the Eastern Cape, came together for two-day study courses. They read parables of Jesus about workers who made a living from the land. Most of the participants were churchgoers and had some level of commitment to the Bible as a revelation of truths about God, but not everyone who took part shared this conviction. In reading the stories together, people found in a text from outside their situation a means of comparison which allowed them to discuss important issues in their own lives.

One particularly striking study from this series was based on the parable of the tenants in Mark 12. The story concerns the owner of a vineyard who sends a number of envoys to collect his share of the produce from some tenant farmers. The tenants, resentful of the owner's demand, variously beat and abuse the envoys, until the owner sends his son, whom they kill. Encouraged to hear the story as a story, without the traditional interpretation – that it concerned God's treatment of Israel, first sending the prophets and then Jesus as the Son who will be killed – the readers related the story to their own experience of being excluded from lands that had traditionally belonged to them. The killing of the owner's son was not seen in terms of the fate of Jesus, but as an understandable but misguided reaction to the fact that the murderous tenants worked hard in the fields only to have a large part of their produce taken from them.

In a traditional reading of the parable, the father and the son become victims against whom a terrible wrong is done. In the contextual reading by South African participants, the son pays a terrible price for the ineffectual behaviour of the father. 'What kind of landowner is this?' was one of the questions asked. Knowing that there was something deeply wrong in this part of his business venture, should he not have gone there himself, rather than sending his envoys? Could he not have foreseen that the violence was escalating, and that his personal intervention was necessary? The father in the story was not seen as an interventionist God trying to call the people back to obedience, but as a weak and cowardly figure, unable to understand or respond adequately to the grievances of his tenants. The participants understood not only the temptation to violence, but also that it would only make the fate of those who perpetrated it worse. The 'quick fix' solution would merely result in their own expulsion from the land and the further impoverishment of their community.

At the time the study took place, there were strong feelings of dissatisfaction that economic promises made at the time of the first democratic elections in South Africa, nearly ten years previously, had not translated into any significant change in the material circumstances of the poorest in the community. There was also anger that rural land had not been transferred back to ownership in the black community. At that time, the eviction of white farmers and the associated violence in Zimbabwe were at their height: the comparison between the parable and that contemporary example seemed compelling. The participants found in the story told by Jesus not a justification for violence, but a warning that unless issues of land ownership were settled in a just and peaceable way, the future stability of South Africa would be under threat. The violent ending of the story brings no solution to serious problems. It does not result in the tenants achieving their ends, but in their loss even of what little they had to sustain their lives. The parable was interpreted as a call to early intervention, to negotiated and peaceable settlement of land issues before resentment and injustice built up to the point where they were out of control. In one of the studies, a participant said, 'Let's go and fetch the councillors from town to listen to this!' One of the outcomes of the study was a discussion about how the participants might become more active in raising the issues surrounding their own position, on land which was owned by people who did not live in their communities.

Making CBS work in the UK

In these examples from contexts outside the UK, something emerges that seems to be important wherever CBS is done. The relating of sacred story to everyday concerns challenges easy distinctions between 'religious' and 'secular', 'sacred' and 'mundane'. In contrast to that in South Africa or Latin America, the Scottish experience of CBS has not focused on political and economic change. Nevertheless, CBS in the Scottish context has been appreciated in a variety of settings, and by people who come from a wide range of Christian traditions and social backgrounds. *What stands at its heart is a willingness to read the Bible, and to find in it connections with ordinary concerns.*

Throughout the history of the Church there have been renewal movements born out of a discovery of the Bible as 'the people's book', as a means to enliven the faith of ordinary members of the community of faith. This view of the place of the Bible in Christian life has been particularly stressed since the sixteenth century within the churches of the Protestant Reformation. The effects of this are not restricted to reading the Bible. Encouraging people to become readers of the text, not reserving it for those who are professional or trained as interpreters, results in faith as a more democratic activity. The history of CBS in Brazil and its flourishing in a range of Roman Catholic and ecumenical groups in Great Britain, alike show that this approach has come to be valued across different traditions.

A common experience of CBS groups is the realization that there is a distinction between 'knowledge' and 'insight'; the life experience of group members enables them to discover the 'freshness' within the text, giving them a framework for inter-pretation that is as vital to the text as the historical informa-tion that might shed light upon its interpretation. In many biblical narratives change comes as a result of an encounter, a realization that conversation brings transformation. Mention has been made of the conversation between Jesus and the Samaritan woman (John 4). Readers of this story were struck by the extent to which both Jesus and the woman were changed through their encounter. A similar example is the story of Moses' encounter with God in the burning bush (Exodus 3). Out of

Finding the power of the text to transform

For a survey of Bible reading in the West of Scotland, one group was visited in a Roman Catholic parish outside Glasgow. A religious sister led the group, who had a good knowledge of the history of the Bible. Participants in the studies valued the knowledge that she sometimes brought to their readings. They did not, however, think that she had a monopoly on the 'right' answers. Their readings, and the connections they made with the concerns of their daily living, were seen as being just as important. The sister's life experience and the sensitivity she had in listening and encouraging people to share their thoughts were the key to leading a successful group. The leader's knowledge could sometimes enhance their insight, but was not the reason why they valued the studies. They found that by studying together they formed significant relationships, and came to discuss things in a deeper way. The studies were 'fresh' because they enabled a kind of conversation that led them into new insights about themselves, and in the case of that particular group, the studies gave them deeper insight into how they believed God was active in their lives.

The group had read the Sunday Gospel readings from the lectionary over a number of years, so that they were used to returning to passages that they had studied before. They observed that their familiarity with the material over time did not stop them finding new insights. By relating the same texts to their changing circumstances, new perceptions were constantly called forth. This brought them a perspective on the way in which God relates to human life; that is, God is always being sought and found afresh as we experience new things. The group saw in this conversational mode of understanding a way of being receptive to God's communication. The Bible was not a 'word from outside', but a constant re-engagement in an ongoing conversation with the other members of the group in which they also tried to discern the voice of God.

isolation and abandonment Moses is transformed through a meeting and encounter with 'the other'.

Similarly, CBS is able to transform through conversation, an encounter with others. It is transforming because it brings participants to a renewed sense of faith, or to an appreciation of something that, through their engagement with the biblical text, they can take on as a deeper personal commitment. Sometimes it allows a reassessment of elements of participants' personal history, enabling greater self-insight or a sense of reconciliation with something in their past that had previously been left unrecognized or was difficult to deal with. Sometimes it allows people to talk about things that, unsure of their significance or unable to express it, they had allowed to remain unspoken for years.

Theology is for everyone

As we have seen, CBS attempts to close the gap between what is generally understood as 'religious' and 'secular'. Some understandings of faith seem to work on the idea that 'religion' is a reserved sphere, with a language and an activity all of its own. However, exploring the relationship between text and lived experience, as happens in CBS, expresses a theological understanding in which religion is not a sphere of life separate from other activities. Talk of God is entirely bound up with the way in which we experience the world around us.

'Theology' is often an off-putting word, suggesting a complex way of thinking which only those who have been trained to use the right language are able to carry out. Yet, as we have seen, in its essence theology is simply talk about God. Part of the work of the Church is to encourage people to become more aware of the ways they find God in the midst of their lives, more confident to reflect and talk about God, more attuned to acting in ways to which they believe God is calling them. We might define theologians as people who are seeking to become more natural in their talk about God, and more committed to bringing their insight about God to the centre of how they act and relate to the world around them.

If this is the case, then the work of CBS is to encourage people in many different situations to place the work of theology at the centre of their lives. One of the insights that came from our international partners is that theologians do not only sit in universities, earning their money by doing research and writing books. Theologians are not only the ordained, those specially called by churches to work in the communities they serve. Theology is the work of the whole people of God.

In contemporary British society, there are concerns in Christian faith communities that it is difficult to talk about God, in a context where people have not been encouraged to express their thoughts about faith in their own words. One source of insecurity within Christian communities is that the stories of the Bible which used to form a kind of common set of narratives from which many people could draw an understanding are no longer widely known. Older participants in CBS express a sense of loss that the common faith and values which formed them are no longer shared even by other generations of their family or by their neighbours. There can therefore be a reticence and a lack of experience in relating daily life to theological understanding.

CBS starts with the reading of a story, and talking about that story. In that way people are enabled comfortably to express their thoughts about theology. Most people are used to relating their experiences in the form of story, and CBS encourages people to share their own stories, to find significance in things that may seem commonplace to them. In building these bridges between the ancient text and contemporary experience, it is

33

hoped that people will become more able to express themselves theologically – not necessarily in terms of using the traditional language of faith and the Church, but in a wider sense of understanding contemporary life within a framework in which God is an active player. At its heart, this is what theology is about.

3

Ways of reading the Bible

What kind of book is the Bible?

In the history of Christianity, there have been differing under-standings of what kind of book the Bible is. Of course, within its pages there are many kinds of writing, and so finding a single description of the Bible is always going to be elusive. However, people will still want to know of CBS what kinds of assumptions we are making about the text of the Bible. What kinds of expectations do we bring when we read it?

CBS does not assume any particular faith position with regard to the Bible. The studies are instead an invitation to people who have strong faith commitments and those who are more tentative in their beliefs to meet and discuss together biblical texts and the important issues that arise from them. In this sense the Bible is looked on as a *classic text*, one which encour-ages conversation, rather than a text which has a single and simple interpretation to be discovered and learned. The studies may make people more biblically aware, more confident that they are equipped to read the Bible.

Sometimes people will encounter attitudes and values expressed in the biblical text which are out of place in the contemporary world. Attitudes towards slavery and gender are examples that readily spring to mind. There is no assumption in CBS that the text can be read straight; that what is contained is automatically correct. There is no assumption that what a text says about the circumstances of one specific time and culture can be easily applied to another. Nor is it taken for granted that where our current experience does not chime with what is found in the text, then there is something lacking in our experience. The Bible has itself been used in history as a justification for practices which we would now recognize as damaging or oppressive, and readers may well find that they resist taking on the perspectives that seem most immediately expressed through the text.

Questioning the story: is Jesus always right?

Jesus himself challenged many of the commonplaces and assumptions of his time; he accepted sinners into his circle, he did not count reputation or appearance as the most important things about a person. However, when the Syro-Phoenician woman approaches Jesus looking for healing for her daughter (Mark 7.24–30), Jesus appears to want to send her away. He appeals to an ethnic categorization that seems unacceptable to contemporary readers: 'It is not fair to take the children's food and throw it to the dogs' (7.27). The woman refuses to be treated by Jesus in the way that Jewish men usually treated women of her racial and religious background. She will not accept his cold disregard of her concern. And in a courageous encounter with Jesus she calls out of him a change of heart that implies that he has altered his attitudes.

In this story we find attitudes of disregard for people of other races which we would not accept, and we might find it shocking that Jesus should have expressed such views. The encounter does not come as a revelation of a simple truth, but causes us to question. What is our attitude towards the woman? What is our attitude towards Jesus? What is it like to hear the story as a woman in our own culture? In our times the language of equality is common, but it is not matched by the reality of daily life in which men and women have roles which are strongly delineated. What is it like to hear this story as a foreigner living in our society which prides itself on tolerance, but which still discriminates in many ways? The Christian story is told in such a way that the ready assumptions we make about 'the way things are' do not go unchallenged. Reading the text opens up the possibility that the particular experiences within a group can be understood from a variety of perspectives, and the voices of those who struggle to make themselves heard can be taken account of.

Different modes of Bible reading

Typically, within the CBS movement, three modes of reading the biblical text have been distinguished:

- reading behind the text
- reading the text itself
- reading in front of the text.

All these modes of reading have advantages and disadvantages, as we shall see. None of them will wholly uncover *the* meaning of the text; in practice any given session may well draw on a mixture of these approaches. The same text can be explored using all these different modes.

Reading behind the text

Here the text is approached from its historical, cultural and sociological context. The aim is to locate the text in its original setting and to understand the problems, hopes and aspirations of those who wrote it. This will then give the group a key to unlock the contemporary relevance of the text: the personal, social and political problems of the text's context may find analogies in our contemporary context. And similarly, what the writer/text was saying in such a context, the way those problems were being addressed, may have something to say to us in our contemporary context.

An example may help. The aforementioned story of the laying of the foundation of the Temple in Ezra 3 after the Israelites' exile in Babylon (a rich text we have used frequently) can be read with a view to establishing its setting in the life of the people of Israel. You do not need a great deal of historical knowledge to do this: it would be helpful if at least one person in the group has read some basic commentary which explains the story's setting in the return from exile in Babylon, but there are clues in the text which most groups will be able to pick up. As the discussion develops it will be possible to feed in more information: the basic story of the exile, the destruction of Jerusalem and the Temple and the circumstances of the return. Also the Persian king Darius' support for this move, the fact that some remained in Babylon and that there continued to be a thriving group of Jews there for many centuries (something that certainly could not be picked up from the text). Once that basic setting has been established, one might ask further questions about the nature of Israel's relationship to the powerful nations surrounding it, about the experience of exile and captivity and the problems of restoration and renewal after national defeat.

At this point the group may well look to contemporary analogies in its attempt to understand the text and its context better. What must it have been like for, say, Germans who were taken off to Russia after the Second World War and lived for many years in captivity? Or for those who remained in

Scandinavia in rather more comfortable circumstances and did not want to return to the very difficult environment of Germany in the immediate aftermath of the war? Moreover, how much light might our contemporary experience as a nation subject to powerful external influences, whether from other nations or from global businesses, shed on Israel's experience of political domination? It is not difficult to see how the original setting of the text can be analysed through such contemporary parallels. And this in turn can now lead the group to a closer examination of their own experience of return and renewal.

It then should not be difficult to allow the discussion to turn to the group's own context and to allow some of the ideas which have developed in the discussion of this ancient story to illuminate their own experience and situation.

There are considerable strengths in such an approach. It can bring a story vividly to life by locating it more firmly in its original setting. Analysing the story by exploring its parallels with contemporary experiences can shed light on it and at the same time help to bridge the gap between its historical setting and our contemporary world. But there are also disadvantages. Such a discussion could become too much of a history lesson and simply get lost in the past. It risks setting someone up as an 'expert' and disempowering or excluding others with less knowledge. Then, rather than the discussion developing as the group tries to bring its insights and experience to bear on this story, it will become more a matter of one or two trying to tell the group what to make of it. In this case it will become less a discussion of the text in question, more a matter of listening to the opinions of a few.

Reading behind the text was an approach much favoured by Latin American basic ecclesial communities. An analysis of the social setting of a given text, often Marxist inspired, would be the springboard for social and political understanding and action.[12] At its best, such an approach could generate a rich discussion of their contemporary context by people who until then had had few means of understanding their wider context and the political forces dominating their lives. Even so, it could lead to dominance by the 'trained reader', whose function then became more that of an instructor whose role was to unlock 'the' social, historical meaning of the text.

In practice, partly because most of its members had been trained in historical-critical studies, and the fact that they were all too likely to get lost in the past, the Scottish CBS group have used this mode of reading rather sparingly. It seems preferable first to read closely what the text has to say, and only later, or incidentally in the course of discussions, to turn to social and historical analysis. Perhaps the time has come for the group to look at the method afresh.

Reading the text itself

This method focuses on the text itself, the words and images, the characters, emotions and styles that can be found within it. In our study sessions, the CBS group have been repeatedly struck by the sheer richness, the compressed nature, of so many biblical texts. There is more to be discovered in terms of detail, of texture, than most of us expect. Taking again the example of Ezra 3, a group may be asked to go through the text, listing all the characters and the references to place. They may trace out the liturgical details in the text, the historical and temporal references, and the emotions recorded. In each case, the end result will be a flip chart covered with detail. Moreover, any of these listings of detail can provide a route into the text, enabling the group to examine the story more closely and to bring out different aspects and emphases.

The pianist Kathryn Stott once said that in preparing for the performance of a piece, she had to decide which of the many musical lines running through it she would seek to bring out. She could not emphasize all equally. Something of the same occurs in reading texts, particularly narrative texts. Any close reading will have to concentrate on certain themes and motifs in the text, to seek to understand them and to bring them into relation to readers' own experience; to enable readers to encompass them, but also allow themselves to be encompassed by them.

To find a group reading closely like this is exciting for two reasons. First, the group sees so much more than an individual would see on his or her own. And second, the group will throw up all sorts of ways of coming at the text. Sometimes the CBS facilitators will offer choices to simplify the process of deciding which approach to the text to follow further. For example, the different characters in a story might be identified, then one of the characters will be selected and the story retold from his or her perspective. On one occasion, during a discussion of the call of Levi, a group decided to retell the story from the point of view of one of the tax collectors. This required a certain amount of historical information about the status and role of tax collectors. What followed was a very interesting discussion of the possible impact of Jesus' open fellowship on the tax collectors themselves. These men, with their ambiguous if powerful position in Jewish society, would have been pulled in different directions by such an invitation to sit down with a popular and somewhat subversive preacher and healer. Here was a way of shedding light on Jesus' statement that he had not come to call the righteous but sinners.

The advantages of this method of reading lie in the way in which it allows readers to concentrate on the text, to open up its various levels of meaning. It slows down our reading of the text, makes us take in its detail and gives us a chance to make its ideas and imagery our own, so that we become equipped with a language in which to discuss our own experiences and dilemmas. In this way it can lead into rich discussions and can assist people in articulating some of their deepest feelings and convictions. For example, the parable of the father and his two sons (Luke 15.1–3, 11–32) is a very familiar story. It needs to be reread in a way that will help us to hear it afresh. It has the potential to release profound insights into readers' own behaviour and the nature of compassion and care, but also into the nature of rivalry and jealousy. Retelling the story from the father's point of view can shed light on his conflicting emotions and the cost of forgiveness and its release. That in turn can lead people to identify similar moments in their own experience and find an understanding of those moments that can bring release.

There are things that this method cannot do. On some occasions a lack of historical knowledge may lead one to misread details in a story based on rural life two thousand years ago. Moreover, our texts are inevitably translations. Pressing on the details may sometimes tell us more about the translation than about the original text (or may tell us about the translator's understanding of the Greek text – which is a construct based on many different manuscripts). On the other hand, if we do not keep to the discipline of looking at the detail and texture of the passage, then there is the danger that we shall end up with a rather superficial or literal interpretation of the text. Nevertheless, although we should look out for such dangers, they do not pose insuperable difficulties. This remains the way of reading that is most accessible for those who have little or no knowledge of the Bible or experience of reading it. It also brings surprising rewards.

Reading in front of the text

This approach brings together a number of ways of reading the text, all of which start with the readers and the interests and concerns they bring to the text. This is where studies which look at particular topics or themes naturally fit in. A group decides that it wants to think about the way it deals with its possessions, its wealth, its use of natural resources, the way it fits into the local community, the way it deals with conflict, and seeks to do so via study of the Bible. How does it go about it?

A wonderfully clear and lucid account of how a number of groups recently read the Bible in this way is given in Louise Lawrence's 2009 book *The Word in Place*. She asked how people thought about the place in which they lived, their homes, their communities, and how they sought to make them better places in which to live. And she did this partly through group activities that helped people to understand the question, and partly through Bible studies.

An example of group activities would be that used with a small group who met with Lawrence in the pub in the Dartmoor village of Drewsteignton. They were simply asked to list various aspects of the community suggested by the letters of its name. In this way a great variety of associations were collected and an awareness of the issues generated. The same ends could be achieved by simply asking people to share experiences of the place they wish to consider.

This kind of approach raises sharply the question about which texts to use. What is most appropriate for any given subject? Lawrence broke the topic into four sub-themes: home, those out of place, sustainability, the call to be displaced. She chose a text for each of these themes. For 'home' she chose the story of the Prodigal Son, Luke 15.11–32; for 'those out of place', the story of Jesus in the Temple, Luke 2.41–52; for 'sustainability', the Stilling of the Storm, Luke 8.22–39; for 'the call to be displaced', Jesus' sayings about discipleship in Luke 9.46–52. The groups who took part reflected on various aspects of their experience of place and retold their stories in the light of these reflections. This led them to value more highly the developments and initiatives that had been undertaken in their communities, to strengthen their support for those developments and to engage more fully with their places and communities.[13]

This is only one way in which one might handle such a thematic, 'in front of the text' approach to reading the Bible. As we saw in Chapter 1, selected psalms of exile were read in studies with churches in the East End of Glasgow. Those particular texts were chosen not least because it was thought that the reflection of suffering expressed within them would be a suitable topic for the period of Lent during which the studies fell. In the event the theme of exile became an important one in its own right. The question of the churches' place within the communities in which they had once had a very central role emerged very strongly. Both the physical destruction of their built communities and the loss of position within the communities that remained made the metaphor of exile a very pertinent one to the ecumenical groups with whom the text was read.

This approach can be broadened out to embrace ways of reading which are more concerned to hear what particular books or sections of the Bible have to say. A group may want to hear what the message of the prophets is, or the Wisdom literature, or may want to take a Gospel or a Pauline epistle and study that. It will be clear that this comes close to the 'reading the text' approach, but it is also driven by concerns which people bring to the text: to hear the message of the prophets in their own particular situation, to improve their understanding and knowledge of the Bible.

This approach, like the others, has its strengths and weaknesses. Its great advantage over the 'reading the text' mode is that it starts much more clearly from a particular set of questions with which the group chooses to work. There is no danger that the reading of the passage will fail to move beyond the study of the passage itself, fail really to impinge on the lives of the readers. Time will be given, probably at the start of the process, to exploring the questions and getting the group to reflect on them.

However, the danger is that there may not be a very close fit between the passages chosen and the issues and questions which people want to address. It is possible that people in the group may expect rather more direct answers to their questions from the passages than is realistic, with the result that the text may be twisted to say things that are fairly far-fetched. These are potential dangers, not insuperable obstacles. Facilitators will need to remind readers that the texts may come from a rather different context than the readers' own and that what the group is suggesting is not what the texts actually say. In this way, there will again be a mixing of the various approaches, as is almost always the case. The point about identifying different ways of reading is that it helps one to plan a particular strategy with respect to any single reading session and at the same time to be aware of other ways of approaching the text, which one may want to draw on where appropriate.

4

Different readers – different meanings

Over the last 30 years or more there has been a significant shift in the way that literary scholars and critics think about the way we understand texts. It once used to be thought that the task of the reader was to discover *the* meaning of a text; now there is much more awareness of the way that readers themselves are involved in constructing meaning when they read. This is partly because the text simply does not provide us with enough information. There are gaps in a narrative, ambiguities in discourse, metaphors and figures of speech that can be construed in different ways.

All these things mean that the reader has to be at work, supplying what is missing, resolving (to his or her satisfaction at least) some of the lack of clarity, allowing the metaphor to suggest various ways of making sense of what is being said. And in carrying out these tasks, readers bring a whole world of experience to the reading of the text. They will emphasize those elements in a narrative or discourse which have particular resonance for them, resolve ambiguities in ways that fit in with their understanding of life and human ways, and this will certainly lead to considerable variety of interpretation.

All this is just as true for the Bible as for any other kind of text. Let us take a well-known contemporary example. A figure like Desmond Tutu, growing up in apartheid South Africa under the influence of Trevor Huddleston, educated at King's College, London, spending much of his life combating an oppressive and racist regime, brings many different kinds of experience to his reading of the biblical text. On the one hand, a tradition of High Church Anglicanism, a mixture of liturgical worship, liberal Catholic scholarship, and a tradition of social and political involvement. On the other, a rich African spirituality and an involvement in a fierce political struggle, led to a significant degree by Marxists, though supported by people of many different political persuasions. When Tutu reads the Bible all these factors and more come to bear. 'I am puzzled which Bible people are reading', he says from an old Christian Aid poster, 'when they say that the Bible and politics don't mix.' Texts in the Bible that talk about political oppression and the abuse of power speak directly to his situation. The story of Naboth's vineyard, where Jezebel talks her royal husband into doing away with Naboth in order to take his property, has direct relevance to the South African regime's forced removals of black South Africans from their ancestral lands. And such arguments could also have an impact on the white South African rulers who were brought up in a particular tradition of the Reformed Church that read the Bible very differently.

In perhaps less dramatic and obvious ways, the same is true when any group of people gather to read a text, biblical or otherwise. In any group there will be people with very different life experiences, cultural, religious and intellectual backgrounds, and with many other different gifts that they will bring to bear on the text. The not inconsiderable task of the facilitators in a CBS group is to recognize such skills, gifts and experience and to allow them to play their part in the conversation which, one hopes, will develop. All of these skills are those that the facilitators

Highland prodigal

A memorable CBS session occurred in a remote Highland village church. The story studied was that of the Father and the Two Sons (Luke 15), one of whom tradition terms 'the Prodigal'. The group explored the theme of people's business being so 'well-kent' in their own small rural community that it was almost impossible ever to be accepted back into the fold after abusive behaviour of any sort, however reformed the perpetrator had become. Labels stick indelibly, they said, and not only to the errant one but to his or her family too. The magnanimity and self-forgetfulness of the father in the story galvanized them into thinking about how *they* could be a community of forgiveness to the local 'black sheep' next time he emerged from the cells after brawling. That is, by helping to reintegrate him into the community and speaking a word of shattering prodigal love into the general atmosphere of enduringly harsh memories.

themselves will be seeking to exercise and model. This does not, however, mean that they are the exclusive preserve of the facilitators. If what one is trying to encourage is a conversation between people seeking meaning in their lives, then these are skills to encourage in all the members. The CBS process is participatory and exploratory; many people come to the study of the Bible expecting to be passive, not expecting to contribute actively to the learning process. But the experience of groups reading in this way can energize people and surprise them, not least as they discover skills they did not know they had. This in turn will generate insight into the texts that they read, whether narrative or discursive. So what sort of skills and gifts is one looking for?

Using the skills of the group

One essential skill is for the facilitators to cultivate an ability to listen and to be genuinely open to all the members of the group. If they underestimate someone, they may all too easily discourage that person from participating as fully as possible. Some of the most original insights may come from members of the group from whom one might least have expected it. It is important to recognize such insight when it is offered and to bring it into the mainstream of the discussion. In practical terms, this may mean making sure that what has been said is written up accurately and perceptively, and also that what is being said is clearly drawn out. Most of the time when someone says something of interest, it will be fairly clear, but sometimes it may be offered in a way which is indirect and tentative.

It is also essential for the facilitators to recognize among the members a variety of skills and insights which can contribute to the most efficient functioning of the group. The following list is based on discussions with people who have participated in CBS training sessions. It is not meant to be exhaustive.

Biblical and theological skills

In the first place, there may be skills and knowledge in the group which are closely related to those used and developed in the academic discipline of biblical studies: skills in understanding the literary, historical and theological dimensions of the biblical writings. All of these can be useful in their place. A good knowledge of the biblical writings and their interconnections can help to place a narrative in its wider context, help in understanding a quotation of a biblical text in a Gospel or epistle. Historical knowledge will help to locate the texts in their original context and contribute something about their importance in the subsequent history of the Church and those societies that have been influenced by the Bible. Equally, people with a theological background can sometimes find the right terms and concepts to give expression to what the group is searching for, can clarify terms and also shed light on people's own theological traditions. Above all they can help the group develop its own theological language.

It will be quite easy to spot people who have these kinds of skills and knowledge. The task of the facilitators is to make sure that such skills are put at the disposal of the group and are used to support and develop the conversation rather than to dominate it. There can be a problem, if someone with, say, particular historical expertise should think that this gives him or her a privileged position in the group. Nevertheless people with such skills and training undoubtedly have their part to play.

The same will be true for other forms of expert knowledge and training. If the application of a text takes the group into a particular field – say, bioethics, the ethics of fair trade, or questions of carbon reduction and sustainable lifestyles – then it can be helpful to have such expertise on hand. Again the point is that such expertise should be at the service of the group, should be made available when asked for, not imposed on the group.

Literary skills

Alongside the biblical, historical and theological skills already discussed, there may also be literary skills that can be quite widely shared. The ability to give a close reading of a text is not a specifically theological skill, but it is one that is most valuable in a CBS group. So much of the Bible needs to be read with an awareness of the complexity of a text, its changes of mood and style, its use of language, the different voices it may contain, the allusions and quotations which may be only hinted at. Some of that may only be accessible to the group member who has a more extensive knowledge of contemporary literary and linguistic conventions.

On the other hand, there will be a great deal that is accessible to the group as a whole, even within a single passage of Scripture. A group of competent and practised readers will be constantly surprised at how much they can find in a text. Again these are skills which facilitators should be cultivating in the group and modelling themselves. It is part of the process of slowing down the reading of any passage so that people can steep themselves in it and begin to pick up and use its language and ideas in order to make sense of their own experience.

People skills

Next, there is a range of people skills that can contribute to the sense of confidence and ease which people have within the group. People who are sensitive to different personalities, who can encourage those who are hesitant and gently rein back those who are overconfident, are good allies for the facilitators. Similarly, there will be those who have good listening skills. These people do not rush to assume that they know what someone is trying to say (and even to contradict it), but will ask for more, for clarification, and will then offer something of their own to draw out its significance. There will also be those who have the ability to challenge and criticize without giving offence, affirming what others have said while offering alternative views and perspectives.

Life skills

Finally, there is a range of personal life skills that can help to open up the meaning of a text for the group. Such skills are

Encouraging active readers

Some models of Bible study are passive. They depend upon the 'expert' giving his or her interpretation of the text, and the audience merely receiving the expert's wisdom. Institutional forms of church often stress the dominance of experts, whether through the hierarchy of the church and its pronouncements, or the special gift of the ordained. However, as we have seen, CBS requires of readers a commitment to use their knowledge in a way that does not imply a position of superiority. The way in which CBS is facilitated is an attempt to break away from talk dominated by certain kinds of formal, approved or institutionally validated experience or knowledge which may be taken to be more highly valued than that of other participants.

Leaders of CBS groups who are ordained should be aware that they need to take special care that the members of the group do not always look to them as the expert who will give them the answers. CBS is facilitated rather than led; the process is designed to allow each participant to feel that he or she has made a personal engagement with the text, and to bring that engagement into a conversation that is shared by the whole group. All members of the group should feel that their contribution is valued.

In many cases, two facilitators share the direction of a session in order to reinforce the idea that no single person has a controlling voice; that no one is bringing his or her knowledge to bear on the rest of the group. The facilitators should instead encourage and enable the insights of the group to be shared, to stop the conversation being dominated by any individual or small group within the study. They should be sensitive to times when one strong personality expresses opinions that are not generally held, and encourage others to say how they feel about what is being discussed. Where there are two facilitators they may sometimes disagree with one another. Their dialogue about what the text means is a model of the kind of conversation that enables other members of the group to see that the text is capable of more than one interpretation. It is often helpful for facilitators explicitly to point out perspectives that they had not thought of prior to the study, showing that they too are learners, and that even the least 'experienced' members of the group have insights which bring fresh understanding.

In CBS, dialogue and the holding of difference, realizing that no one single interpretation exhausts all the possible meanings of the text, are encouraged. The emphases on process and on the valuing of difference are central to what CBS aims to achieve.

perhaps furthest removed from the academic competencies associated with study of the Bible. For example, the ability to draw on and to reflect on one's life experience to illuminate the text; someone who is able to bring up an incident from their life, which has interesting parallels with a textual example, can bring great light into a discussion. Note that in one sense this is a basic historical skill: if a scholar cannot find analogies between his or her own situation and the situations he or she is attempting to understand, there will be little progress. Again, a sense of humour may often illumine a text, picking out some of the tone of a story or debate that would otherwise go unnoticed. A lively imagination can be of great use in reconstructing a narrative, to build up a mental picture of the context. Lastly, there is emotional intelligence, the ability to identify and interpret the emotional tone and quality of a narrative or debate.

This list of skills, although by no means exhaustive, should alert the facilitators to the potential of a group. The facilitators may not share all of these skills. Some will be more, some less relevant to their particular gifts. However, all these characteristics are capable of lifting a discussion on to a new level, if used thoughtfully and to further the quality of the conversation.

Reading through the eyes of another

It is important not to overlook or undervalue the kinds of skills and gifts that are more generic, more related to life skills, more based on particular types of experiences. 'To read the Bible with the poor and marginalized,' said the members of the ISB who first fired the imagination of people in Glasgow, 'can be a life-transforming experience.' It can certainly enlarge the person you are. You begin to see the Bible 'through the eyes of another' and this is transformational, it makes you someone different.

Hans De Wit's intercultural project, 'Through the Eyes of Another', threw up many interesting examples of this. One concerned a group in post-apartheid South Africa, paired with a group in Colombia. The South Africans, predominantly a group of white people from the Reformed Church, read the story of the Samaritan woman at the well as an invitation to do something for African women walking long distances in the bush to collect water. The Colombian group, office workers in a busy city, saw it as being about their relationship to the urban poor, who came into their offices to clean shoes or who accosted them on the streets. They were very much aware of the dangers of such encounters, and how delicate even the relationships with the shoe cleaners could be. They felt that this text was calling them to run those risks and to reach out over the social boundaries to meet and engage with such people. When the South African group read the

> Colombians' interpretation, they were clearly moved. They acknowledged that in their reading they had not really thought about the women walking across the veldt as their sisters but as objects of charity – at a safe distance. And they resolved to change.
>
> In the same way, in any group, hearing the text reflected through someone else's eyes, viewed through their experience, reflected on with their particular wisdom and insight can bring fresh understanding.

The value of folk-readings

Discussions about the relationships between different types of readers in the CBS process have sometimes focused heavily on the relationship between the leaders of the group and the other members. In Gerald West's discussion, this was spoken of as the relationship between the 'trained' reader and the 'ordinary' reader. There were a number of reasons for focusing the discussion in this way. First, in the working groups associated with the Institute for the Study of the Bible, the differences between readers with a formal academic training in theology and the poor and marginalized groups with whom they worked in the townships was undoubtedly large. It was necessary to reflect on how to manage the relationship between those with a formal training and those with none. Second, CBS in both Latin America and South Africa had put a great deal of emphasis on historical and sociological readings of the biblical texts and this clearly meant that those with training in such disciplines would have an interpretative advantage.

This is less of an issue within the British context, partly because the educational differences are not nearly as extreme, partly because the CBS group have worked hard not to privilege particular kinds of knowledge. We stress that although such knowledge may be drawn on as a resource for the group as required, it is not something that should determine the course of the conversation or confer a particular authority on any participant. Insight is as important as knowledge.

In her 2009 book *The Word in Place*, Louise Lawrence prefers therefore to avoid talk of trained and ordinary readers and instead to speak about 'folk-readings'. This is a way of trying to valorize the readings of people without (necessarily) any formal theological qualifications, and of suggesting that there are traditions and forms of wisdom such groups can draw on which are of value in their own right. It is an important step on the road to giving a more positive account of the gifts such readers bring to the texts. But we want to go beyond this and acknowledge both the varieties of gifts that all readers bring to the reading of texts and the variety of sources of such gifts. In a world of mass education there are reading skills widely available that can be harnessed most impressively in a group situation. Equally, with the varieties of education and training available in an affluent democracy (for all its inequalities of wealth), we can expect, as we have said, to find various forms of knowledge at our disposal in any given group which may well help to elucidate issues that arise out of the text.

This is a different situation from that which one might find in more traditional types of society, where there would be far greater reliance on inherited forms of knowledge and wisdom. In this sense we have moved further away from our folk traditions and to a considerable degree lost touch with traditional forms of wisdom. The churches remain in some ways repositories of such traditions, to which, however, those who visit them are often attached quite loosely. They may move freely between one denomination and another, searching for the kinds of meaning that can help them make sense of their life experience.

The very fact that many of the readers at CBS sessions expressed satisfaction at discovering ways of making sense of the Bible suggests that they were people more in search of meaning than looking to impart it. This does not imply that people living in our much more mobile society are bereft of insight. Rather, that the traditions to which they are heir and the insights that they have accumulated are in some ways more fragmentary, less part of a cohesive and communally preserved tradition than would have been the case 100 or even 50 years ago. Again, the task of the facilitator is to be alert to such insight and to bring it out into the group's conversation. In this way a shared discourse can be forged which can assist the group in its continuing search for meaning.

5

Running a Contextual Bible Study

Contextual Bible Study has a simple format: a short time of prayer to begin the session; reading and discussion of the Bible, sensitive to God's transforming word spoken in that group at that time; and a final session of collective prayer. This chapter describes how to run a CBS session, outlining the separate stages involved. It is divided into four sections, each reflecting an aspect of the CBS process, and ends with a last-minute checklist for facilitators. The four sections are as follows:

- setting the scene
- praying and reading aloud
- discussing the Bible passage together
- facilitating the group.

1 Setting the scene

A CBS session is straightforward to organize and requires few resources. The process can be adjusted to work with any size of group, whether three or four people or several hundreds. Yet each group size raises practical considerations for the facilitators. With large groups the CBS process works most easily if you have enough people to break out into groups of three and re-form into a full group. A very small group needs to be facilitated as a full group all the time. A large group requires sensitivity to those who are hard of hearing or who speak quietly. Larger groups need larger spaces; on the other hand, there is a risk that a small group will feel lost in a big hall.

Each of the Bible studies offered in this book is likely to last for about an hour and a half. It is important that the facilitators create an atmosphere that will be helpful for the session. Regarding the group dynamic, this means establishing a sense of trust and mutual respect among the participants. It also includes creating a welcoming, positive environment where the study can take place. Here are some suggestions for facilitators as to what preparation will be needed before the study begins:

- The following should be provided: chairs to sit on, copies of the Scripture passage and questions, and a flip chart and pens for the facilitators.
- It is helpful to arrange the chairs in a circle, with a clear view of the flip chart.
- A prayerful atmosphere can be created by setting up a visual focal point on a low table or on the floor in the middle of the circle – an open Bible, a candle, a piece of coloured cloth.
- If you are serving refreshments, have them ready about half an hour before the starting time.
- Always start on time; latecomers can quietly join the circle as they arrive.
- Give a very brief introduction of yourself and what the session will be about. If the participants are new to each other, invite them to introduce themselves in turn to the others in the group. This can also be a good time to remind everyone that their sharing during the session is confidential to the group.

2 Praying and reading aloud

Opening and closing prayers

Each study begins and ends with a short prayer. Facilitators are encouraged to choose prayers that will suit their group; the sessions can be enriched with different texts and styles of prayers from across the Christian tradition.

The Scripture passage

It is very helpful to provide each participant with an identical copy of the Bible passage being explored, preferably on a single A4 page. This encourages the group members to focus on the chosen passage rather than becoming sidetracked by other passages, related or unrelated.

There is no right or wrong version or translation of the Bible to use for a CBS session. You could choose a version with which your group will be familiar; on the other hand, sometimes an unfamiliar version can prompt fresh insights into a well-known passage. However, it is most useful to explore the text using only one version of Scripture at a time. This helps the group to focus on the meaning of that passage, rather than upon the differences between various translations.

Reading the Scripture passage aloud

It is helpful to read the text aloud together at least once, perhaps twice, before beginning to discuss the questions. There are numerous different options for reading, any of which can enhance the session:

- The text may be read by a single voice, and repeated by another.
- The passage may be divided into sections for two or three readers.

- The group may read round the circle, each member taking a verse at a time.
- The whole group may read the passage together in unison.
- The text may be separated out, like a drama, into the characters and a narrator.

Remember, however, that not everyone feels comfortable reading aloud in public. Always give participants the choice not to read aloud. For example, if you are inviting the group to read the passage round the circle, you could say, 'If for any reason you do not feel comfortable reading out loud in the group, gently nudge the person next to you and they will read on.' This leaves everyone free to read or not, at their own discretion. If you are asking someone to read a longer or more complicated passage, it is helpful to allow them time beforehand to prepare.

3 Discussing the Bible passage together

After the passage has been read, the group will begin discussing the questions. The process works most easily if, at different times in the session, people are invited to break into groups of three for discussion, and then to re-form into the full group to feed back. This is a pattern which allows maximum participation to all those attending the session. In the Bible studies in Part Two of this book, there is an indication beside each question of when people may be asked to reflect on their own, when to work in threes and when to work as a full group. However, this is merely a guide; you are welcome to adapt the plan as best suits the needs of your group.

Some groups work best when each participant has a copy of the question sheet; it can be helpful for members of the group to see in advance how the session can be expected to progress.

The Bible study sessions offered in this book may be reproduced as many times as required. However, with some groups the facilitators may need to adapt the material as the session unfolds; in this case, it would not be useful to hand out the questions at the beginning of the study.

The sessions offered in this book share a common pattern; the questions for discussion generally follow this sequence:

- opening
- close reading
- reflecting on the text and its context
- resonance between the text and the contemporary context
- seeking transformation.

Opening

The opening question begins the conversation within the group. It simply asks for the initial thoughts and feelings of each participant on hearing the text. This question is as open as possible: 'What jumps off the page at you?' Participants are invited to share their reactions to the passage: single words, theological insights, comments about the characters, personal experiences. Everything is welcome; nothing need be discussed in depth or analysed further at this stage.

The participants will have come to CBS with different levels of knowledge and experience. Some will be encountering biblical materials for the first time. Others may be very familiar with the Bible as a whole and with the particular texts that are being read. This means that for some the sense of reading something fresh and unknown will be the point of entry. Others may feel that they are reading texts that have been very familiar to them over a long time, that they 'know what they mean'.

Readers unfamiliar with the text are capable of asking questions which might otherwise be missed, or not expressed because the more experienced think they are too obvious. The question about what jumps off the page is designed to help people come to the text as equals, without regard for their previous knowledge. Whatever anyone says is a correct answer for that person. This question puts everyone on the same footing, because all the impressions are equally valid.

Readers who are steeped in the Bible should be encouraged to see things that had been missed before. For this latter group of readers the question 'What jumps off the page at you?' will be an aid to reading a familiar text as though for the first time. They should try to listen for something new, even to pick up something familiar that seems to be specially relevant to issues that they are facing in their own lives, or are important for the group, or relate to events in wider society. Readers are encouraged to give up their presuppositions to see if something unexpected emerges.

Close reading

Close reading questions are designed to slow down the reading of the group, to allow the participants to discover more of the details and the richness of the text. For example, 'naming' questions ask readers to list the scenes, characters or emotions that may be found within the passage. Later in the discussion, some of these may be explored further.

Reflecting on the text and its context

The members of the group are next invited to consider in more depth some of the key ideas, themes or characters. At this point participants might also be asked to share what they know about the historical, religious or social context of the passage. Often, there will be considerable knowledge available within the group; with judicious questioning, group members will be able to offer this, rather than being 'taught' directly by the facilitator.

Seeking resonance between the text and the contemporary context

The focus of the session now moves from the Bible text into the present experience of the group members. These questions often ask the group to think about ways in which their shared reflection on the passage might shed light on particular contemporary concerns.

Seeking transformation

The next questions affirm and challenge the group in its faith-in-action. For example, such questions ask what difference the members' reflection might make to their personal, church community and wider local community life. Spending time together on this part of the process may help the group to discern practical, communal action for their good and for the good of those around them.

4 Facilitating the group

The facilitators have an enabling role. It is their responsibility to create an accepting, non-threatening atmosphere for the study, so that everyone can take a full part in the session according to their own ability. Facilitators encourage respectful listening and sharing; they discourage disputation, aggression or conflict. It is also up to them to keep participants focused on the topic and to prevent the discussion from being dominated by one or a few people in the group.

Facilitators think in terms of inviting people into the discussion; they are not expected to know all the answers themselves. Open questions encourage dialogue and exploration. Listening can be more valuable than talking. Not everyone has had experience of group discussion; not everyone feels comfortable talking aloud. Yet all will be reflecting and participating with the group at some level.

One of the challenges of this approach to reading the Bible is how to encourage the exploration of a text and manage the dynamics of the group without 'setting the agenda' for the participants. Although there cannot be such a thing as an unbiased reading of Scripture, facilitators actively try not to impose their own issues or interpretations on others. However, this does not mean that they must not ask searching questions; on the contrary, sometimes the group may need their help to clarify particular areas of difficulty or challenge. Sensitivity and experience are needed here. The following are some recommendations of good practice for CBS facilitators.

Working in teams

Working as a pair or a team of facilitators is strongly recommended. It allows the facilitators to share the responsibilities, the difficulties and the joys of running the study. In particular, it is much easier for two people to monitor the progress of the session and to make any necessary adjustments.

Being sensitive to the group

Observe the group continually, being aware of people's body language as well as what they say. Remember to refer back to the group: are they ready to move on to another question? Is clarification required of a point that has been made? Continually invite people to join in the session, with encouraging words, expressions and gestures.

Using open questions

Open questions are questions that do not presume an answer. They solicit a personal response, and require that response to be respected – even when it may be gently challenged or developed further by the group. Open questions may ask, 'What do you know about . . . ? What do you feel . . . ? Why do you think . . . ?' By contrast, 'closed' questions look for the 'right' answer in the mind of the questioner; they may simply invite 'yes' or 'no' responses. Closed questions reduce the level of participation in a group, especially if members feel that they lack some expert knowledge.

Hearing all contributions

The CBS process aims to encourage all the members of the group to participate as best they can, without any one person dominating – including the facilitators. So as to involve every-body in discussing the questions, it is useful to subdivide the group into smaller groups, threes or pairs, inviting a reporter from each subgroup to give feedback to the full group. It may be that some people have wider or more specialist knowledge, biblical or otherwise, which is relevant to the study. Their input should be welcomed as a gift to the whole group. The facilita-tors need to make sure, however, that this does not overwhelm the session; that other participants do not feel disempowered by the expertise of a few.

Coping with difficult discussions

Sometimes group discussions develop in such a way as to challenge even the most experienced and confident facilitator. However, there are some easy-to-use techniques which may be helpful in such situations. If you see that someone has expressed an opinion that is not widely shared, rather than simply hear-ing and recording that contribution, it could be opened up to the group. Say, for example: 'Thank you for raising this . . . there may be other ways in which members of the group would like to deal with this . . . What do others think?' The influence of a disruptive participant can also be ameliorated by breaking the group up into threes as often as possible and by one of the facilitators joining the small group with that person.

Affirming the members of the group

The best sessions are those where the facilitators have confidence in the group and enjoy their company. The facilitators should never hurt anyone with a critical put-down; indeed, the most feisty and talkative participants may be especially vulnerable. Honour their contributions, then widen the discussion to the whole group: 'What do others think ... ?' Everyone should leave a CBS session feeling valued and worthwhile.

Keeping to time

This is an important consideration; the facilitators' care over timekeeping is an expression of their respect for the group. Before each session, plan how much time will be allotted to each of the questions. If you do not trust yourself to stick to the plan, appoint someone in the group to be the timekeeper for each exercise.

Recording on the flip chart

Using a flip chart to record the discussion during a CBS session means that ideas can be revisited and explored further as the study progresses. Try to capture each participant's exact wording: people respond well to seeing their contributions honoured in this way. The completed sheets can be displayed on the walls or spread out on the floor for all to see. Sometimes, however, it may not be appropriate to write up contributions; for example, when personal stories are being shared. If in doubt, consult the group about whether they would like their sharing to be recorded or not.

Writing up after a session

Some groups find it useful to have their flip chart feedback typed up and distributed to them for reference after the study. This may particularly assist a group involved in a long-term project or discernment process. In such cases, the facilitators and the group will agree during the session on how much writing up is to be done.

Last-minute checklist for facilitators

Planning beforehand

- What roles will be taken by each facilitator?
- What time will the session begin and end?
- How will the Bible passage be read aloud?
- How long will be spent on each question?

Materials to take

- Prayers to open and close the session
- Copies of the Bible passage
- The CBS questions
- Flip chart and pens

Setting up the room

- Refreshments served half an hour before the study begins
- A circle of chairs with a clear view of the flip chart
- A prayerful focal point in the centre of the circle

6

Real-life stories: CBS in action

What is CBS like in practice? This chapter offers two case studies. The first is a detailed account from an ecumenical church group in Glasgow, Scotland's largest city. The second describes a number of sessions with larger groups, focusing particularly on a session conducted in a secondary school and giving an account of what happens when CBS and teenagers are thrown together. These stories are offered with the thought that CBS is a highly adaptable method of allowing the Bible to speak, and encouraging people of all ages and contexts to engage in discussion with and around it. Difference of background, faith commitment and, importantly, size of group need not be an obstacle. Our hope is that new ways and styles of deploying the CBS method will continue to emerge and that these will encourage others to discover its strengths and their own developing strengths as its practitioners.

CBS at a church in Glasgow

An ecumenical group, drawn from a number of churches across the West End of Glasgow, met together at St Bride's Episcopal Church in March 2007 for a series of four studies on the Gospel readings for Lent. As many as 18 and no fewer than 14 people from six different churches attended each study. Exclusively churchgoers, most but not all of the participants were already acquainted with the CBS method. There was an equal balance of men and women in the group.

Although they varied in age from those in their thirties to those in their eighties, on the whole the group was elderly. Many did not live particularly close to the church; some had infirmities. For these people, coming out in the evening, braving the dark and the inclement West of Scotland weather, was an act of faithful devotion in itself. The host church is situated on the Hyndland Road, in a late nineteenth-century residential suburb of four-storey tenements and large town houses, many of which have been converted into flats. The area has a transient population: there are groups of students sharing flats, and young professionals, some with children; yet there are also elderly people, who have lived in the same tenement apartment for 20, 30, perhaps 40 years.

St Bride's Church is a red sandstone Edwardian building, whose quasi-medieval presence, with heavy, thickset tower, looms at the side of the busy main road. The life of the congregation is largely defined by its distinctively 'high', ritualistic form of worship. A lively CBS group was established there in 2003 and had been meeting regularly for four years at the time of this Lent series. We convened in the church crypt, a large yet unexpectedly awkward space: it proved almost impossible to arrange the room with a comfortable circle of chairs, all with a good view of the flip chart, because of the great pillars holding up the floor of the church above. During the day the crypt housed a nursery school, whose cheery handiwork covered the walls. The mostly elderly CBS members sat on brightly coloured plastic chairs, surrounded by the detritus of the very young. Tea, coffee and cakes were served beforehand; there was time for chatting and fellowship. We took care to start promptly, however, and – especially important to this group – we finished promptly, for safe journeying home.

1 Are we nearly there yet?

The first of the passages for discussion seemed to be just a scrap of Scripture, a mere five verses. Luke 13.31–35 describes an encounter of Jesus with some Pharisees during his journey to Jerusalem. The group was struck by the variety of contrasting figures in this short passage: foxes and hens, Jesus and the Pharisees, Jesus and Herod, demons and the sick, Jerusalem and the prophets. These relationships were generally negative, yet not exclusively so. Jesus' relationship with Jerusalem was described as maternal; his manner to the sick was kind and compassionate. The Pharisees seemed particularly interesting: it was far from clear what motivated them to approach Jesus. Were they trying to warn him? Were they spies, or messengers from Herod? One person observed that in Greek, a messenger was an angel.

The group considered the incident from the Pharisees' point of view. It was understandable that they did not want Jesus to reach Jerusalem; in volatile first-century Judaea, his presence might potentially lead to conflict, with both the Jewish and the Roman authorities. As a group member remarked, 'All the political and religious authorities just wanted Jesus to go away.' They were more than simply the stereotypical 'baddies' of Christian tradition. The group recognized that there were sometimes occasions when they too were tempted to wish that Jesus would 'go away'. One person offered his personal experience, of a time in which he had felt confused: he had not been sure if he was 'on the side of Jesus or on the side of Herod'. He had been angry with someone, yet eventually he realized the urgency of forgiveness in that situation.

Some time was spent reflecting upon the character of Jesus and his role in the story. He was perceived as determined, firm of purpose, 'no shrinking violet'. He was insightful; he understood the Pharisees, he could see through Herod, he had no illusions about Jerusalem. Moreover, he was a complex individual: even in these few verses, he exhibited a range of emotions, including disgust, doggedness, sorrow and compassion. He seemed supremely confident in his 'monumental purpose', and completely obedient to God. One person remarked upon the incomprehensibility of Jesus and of the text; we may think that we know something about Jesus and the New Testament, but to an extent, they remain 'unknowable'.

However, the group felt it was helpful to compare the strong character of Jesus to determined people in history and in our own time. There are people today who risk everything for their beliefs. It is unusual for anyone to suffer death for their convictions in modern Britain, yet there are parts of the world where people do suffer thus, and often we forget about them. The strong leadership of Jesus was explored further, in relation to the group's understanding of leadership in general, and to particular examples of leaders. Such figures may act as prophetic voices, their criticism of society being important to its development in particular times and situations. One such example was William Wilberforce: he came easily to mind because of the 200th anniversary of the 1807 Act to abolish slavery.

On the one hand, the group realized how fatuous it might seem to place a man like Wilberforce, however worthy, alongside Jesus, the Son of God. Nevertheless, they felt it was still helpful to contemplate examples of strong leaders who 'move people and society along' for good, especially those prophetic leaders who risk everything in the face of 'principalities and powers' which are far larger than individuals. The group pondered whether the circumstances throw up the right person to meet the needs of the time, or whether the person appears, ready to speak to the situation? Such questions may not easily be answered; however, that time was right for Jesus.

Jesus' compassion for the sick and his yearning for the people of Jerusalem prompted a discussion about the mission of the Church, the body of Christ in the world. Connections were made between the New Testament context and the group's own context. In the Pharisees' Judaea, socio-political and religious structures were closely linked. In Scotland, the churches were once used to exercising considerable power and authority in society: now they are much diminished, there is a looser relationship between the state and religious groups. Jesus' concern for the needs of the sick is a feature of this passage. Historically, the churches had a crucial role in ministering to the sick, but in our own society, the state is expected to care for such people.

However, it was felt that the churches still have a very important role to play. After all, the state cannot offer people loving friendships which fulfil a deep human need. Caring communities cannot be created by the state. One member of the group cited the example of a small evangelical church in the neighbourhood near her home. It was not a church she attended herself, but she was aware that the congregation was working locally with needy young people, in very positive ways. This was recognized as a good example of Christians making a Christ-like impact. In recent times, some church communities have felt themselves enfeebled by their lack of numbers and by financial constraints; such perceived shortcomings present obstacles when congregations try to respond to 'prophetic voices' or reach out to the community. Yet even very small churches can and do overcome these obstacles, and reach out lovingly to those around them. This was perceived to be a challenge, and was felt keenly by some members of the group.

2 Big questions and hard answers

The second passage, Luke 13.1–9, elicited uncomfortable feelings of foreboding: the mention of Pilate in the first verse threw a prophetic shadow over this Lent reading. The members of the group felt curious: they were familiar with the parable of the fig tree, but less so with the disaster narrative preceding it. It did not seem immediately clear how to connect that narrative with the parable. Yet they were not discouraged: although it sometimes seemed that Jesus deliberately made his parables obscure, consequently they could mean different things to different people. There was a freedom in parables, a message for everyone. The group would remember the story, and thinking it over, might receive fresh insights later. One person wondered: where was God in this story? No explicit mention of him was found in the text. However, the group found images of God in the parable: God as the owner of the vineyard, disappointed in the tree, yet patient and forbearing to judge. 'Manure' was an unconventional yet striking metaphor for God's nurturing and transforming grace.

They wondered about the fruit that the tree was expected to bear. The cycle of violence described in verse 1 bore no fruit at all. Some in the group understood the fig tree to be a metaphor for Israel. Israel had become bitter and angry; murderous factions committed outrages, which in turn led to Roman repression. By behaving thus, the fig tree could be said to be handing an axe to its destroyer. The cycle of violence perpetuated by the rebels of Galilee bore no fruit, but elsewhere in the Gospels, Jesus taught people to turn the other cheek and bless those who persecuted them. So the parable points to an opportunity for communal as well as personal repentance and transformation.

74

Jesus told his fig tree story in response to the news events current at that time; the group explored ways in which the passage might relate to their contemporary world. Someone described having been shocked that very morning by a newspaper story about gratuitous police violence. The question of human trafficking was raised; it had been much in the media lately. St Bride's Church had been holding a weekly vigil in Lent for the victims of modern-day slavery; was this kind of Christian concern a 'bearing fruit'? Aggressive international trading practices were mentioned, as were the cruelties to animals caused by intensive farming. Could countless small Christian acts 'bearing fruit' in these circumstances ever change the policies of governments and industries?

Whereas in Jesus' day the Galilean insurgency and the collapse of a tower in Siloam were topical, for the CBS group, the insurgency in Iraq and global warming seemed especially pressing. The recent waves of bombing and kidnapping in Iraq seemed to mirror the political violence of the story in Luke's Gospel, with competing groups struggling against foreign military occupation. One person compared the owner of the fig tree to British and American foreign policy makers, who seemed to be saying to Iraq, 'We'll give you another year, and then we're off!' Others wondered, 'Why waste manure on this fig tree?' They then compared Iraq's situation with the peace process in Northern Ireland, where trust was very slowly built up and old enemies learned to work together. By the 'manure' of God's grace, there could be change for good.

Although they were earnestly concerned, the war in Iraq had not personally touched anyone in this CBS group. They felt, however, that global climate change affected everyone. All Christians must think about it, as the problem would not go away. They described the consequences in rather apocalyptic terms: 'If we don't act, we shall be cut down,' remarked a member of the group. Unless there was change in human behaviour, they predicted, 'Nature will take drastic action.' God's own creation, horribly distorted by selfish, careless humankind, would be the axe that cut them down – a ghastly deforestation of those who deforested.

A more personal reading of the passage was offered by some in the group. Meditating on the fall of the tower in Siloam, they remarked that, as Jesus described, sudden disasters are still associated with sinfulness. One person remembered reactions of that kind to the Boxing Day Asian tsunami. Misfortunes in life nurture feelings of sin, and a sense that 'God is punishing you.' Yet Jesus contradicted this view in the Gospel passage. Why then the tower had fallen on some rather than others, the group did not explore further. Indeed, their attitude was stoical; accidents and misfortunes would be inevitable; death might come suddenly. However, they did not want to have lived wasted 'barren fig tree' lives. They were comforted to know that God is patient, and that there was still time to bear fruit.

3 A father and two sons

Reading the parable of the lost son (Luke 15.1–3, 11–32) together evoked strong feelings in members of the group, who had already connected this story with particular times in their own lives. During the previous week's study, the group's reflection on the fig tree parable had led to discussions which ranged widely across issues of global magnitude. This week, the discussion was rooted in the profoundly personal. Indeed, the group's reading of the passage was defined by their experience of human relationships, especially within the family. They agreed that this parable has considerable and enduring appeal; after all, children still squander their parents' money, siblings are still jealous, parents still forgive their children and welcome them home. Someone shared the story of a family whose daughter had gone away and become addicted to drugs; they had taken infinite care to bring her back and help her to stay away from drugs. The person telling that story, and the group listening, recognized how important it had been when, like the son in the story, the daughter reached the point when she wanted to come back.

This parable was a good story, 'a cracking yarn'. The family fights reminded the group of a soap opera; the description was so vivid that 'you can almost smell the meat roasting'. As the group considered the actions of the different characters in this passage, they were struck less by the improvident recklessness of the younger son than by the grumbling of the scribes and Pharisees. Their displeasure at Jesus, welcoming sinners, was mirrored in the story by the grumbling of the elder brother. Some people in the group suggested that the elder brother had been treated unfairly and that his reaction was natural; after all, the younger brother had taken his share, deserted the family and squandered the money. And the father had also abandoned the proper rules of family life; his behaviour to his younger son did seem excessively generous.

The father's excessive generosity was further explored as the group discussed where God was to be found in the passage. The father's complete acceptance of the son was an expression of his love; nothing that we can do will make God love us any less. Like the father, God gives us the freedom to do what is wrong, but he looks out for the lost, and his love reaches out to them: 'he deals', said a member of the group, 'with people as they need it.'

This led to a reappraisal of the behaviour of the elder brother. Like the Pharisees, he understood the world according to a strongly developed sense of what was right. However, Jesus embodied the mercy of God, reaching out freely and in compassion. The group perceived that this story was about Jesus and the Pharisees: Jesus was inviting them to join in God's inclusive feast. If they could not participate in the excessive love of God, which offers the joy of a new life to even the most wretched people, then they would 'exclude themselves from the party'.

'We start off demanding justice,' one person remarked, 'but we come back needing mercy.' The Gospel phrase 'When he came to himself' (v. 17) seemed to be pivotal. There have been turning points in all of our lives, when we looked for God – and he ran to meet us. The Pharisees and the elder son had not yet 'come to themselves', but they might yet do so. Although, by the end of the story, it was the elder son who seemed lost, while the younger was found, the father loved and wanted both of them: the group felt strongly that anyone could come to God and be accepted by him. They commented, 'This should be called "the parable of the loving father".'

The overwhelmingly masculine imagery of the parable concerned some of those present: no women were mentioned in the story at all, though perhaps some were implied in the younger son's 'riotous living' (v. 13). They compared the metaphor of God as father with the maternal imagery of the hen with her brood of chicks, which had been discussed during the first Bible study of the series (Luke 13.34). However, when they began to think about occasions when they or people they knew had been challenged to come to their senses, or to forgive someone and welcome that person back, the group had plenty of stories to tell, of mothers as well as fathers. One mother shared her own poignant experience of rejected parental love: 'Sometimes sons have to go through this journey' before they can come back and understand. She had had to lay aside her feelings of hurt before she could let her boy know of her continuing love. Love meant accepting her son and listening to him as a prelude to their reconciliation. The group acknowledged that this took courage and self-control. And, as someone remarked, 'We love because God loved us first.'

It seemed most natural for this group, many of whom were parents with grown-up children, to reflect on their experiences in terms of the father in the parable, rather than any of the other characters. Yet as the session drew to a close, they ruefully agreed that, at one time or another, to some extent, they had behaved like the father, like the younger son and also like the elder son. Reflecting on the parable, they felt hopeful for the future; for, as a member of the group remarked, 'The story was left open for the sinners, the disciples and the Pharisees to fill in what would happen on the next day.'

4 Anointing at Bethany

The final passage, John 12.1–8, prompted further reflections on the theme of family life, because this was the story of a supper party, at the house of Martha, Mary and Lazarus. This was a family that meant a very great deal to Jesus. The group noticed that Martha was the one working; they intuited that making and serving dinner would have been very important to her. Someone pointed out that the entire passage is about service. Martha's service is taken for granted. Much more striking is Mary's extraordinary act of service to Jesus: this is an act of love and devotion, a feminine act. The group acknowledged the intimacy of this moment, expressed through the significance of smell and touch. They wondered how Mary felt when Judas criticized her.

Honourable acts of service performed by Martha and Mary were in marked contrast to the 'bad stewardship' of Judas. He inserted himself into the intimate moment of anointing as a self-proclaimed champion of the poor. The group was keen to explore Judas' role further: some wondered whether he had been misrepresented. Indeed, throughout the Bible study series, this group showed a marked determination to rescue Gospel villains from their stereotypes and, if possible, to rehabilitate them: the Pharisees who featured in the earlier studies, the jealous elder brother of the parable, and now Judas. Here they considered that Judas had a legitimate complaint, since he had a special responsibility to the poor. Some went further; they suspected that the accusation that Judas was a thief had been added subsequently, to blacken his name. But perhaps he had betrayed Jesus, not because of greedy motives, but because he had become disillusioned, and Jesus' behaviour during this supper party hardened his disillusionment.

The discussion about Judas' imminent betrayal of Jesus encouraged the group to think more about images of death in this passage. They remarked upon the figure of Lazarus. He had recently been dead; now he was sitting at the supper table with Jesus' friends. One person wondered whether the costly perfume had been left over from Lazarus' funeral obsequies. Here Jesus was being anointed as if for death, though he was alive – and Lazarus was alive, yet he was someone who had been dead. Lazarus is uniquely indebted to Jesus; the group observed that Lazarus acknowledged this, allowing Jesus to act as the head of his household and to defend his sister from Judas' accusation. Uniquely indebted, and also possessing a unique perspective: they reflected that Jesus was journeying towards death, whereas Lazarus had returned from death. Thus the latter shared with Jesus a 'secret awareness' of what lay beyond the grave, which none of the others had.

Death and preparation for death were themes that seemed to dominate this Gospel passage. And with Lent drawing to a close, members of the group interpreted the presence of Lazarus in this story as predictive of Jesus' approaching death. They thought that Mary's anointing of Jesus was a sign, not only of her love, but also that she accepted that he would die. Being able to think about death and accept it, they thought, allowed her to celebrate Jesus as he was, there and then, in life.

Meditating further on Mary's act of anointing, the group continued to develop the theme of 'service' in the passage. They wondered whether the anointing pointed to Mary's ability to continue Jesus' ministry to the poor in the future. The poor would be served better by her quiet, loving hospitality than by Judas' officiousness. It was suggested that Jesus' remark, 'you will always have the poor with you' (v. 8), was not intended to be dismissive of the poor. Rather, it was a challenge: each of the people who heard him, and we too, by implication, must decide how to carry on Jesus' work. Mary's example showed true service, bringing dignity and life. One person observed that Mary would always see Jesus in the poor from then onwards, and when ministering to them, would remember him.

The action of Mary, the reaction of Judas reminded the group about stewardship in church life. Churches have property and money in banks. They are naturally concerned with looking after these, and maintaining the smooth running of the liturgical year. Christian people may become so preoccupied with administering such things that their mission is diminished: they have become like Judas. Some congregations convince themselves that they are too hard up to bother with the poor; they need their money for themselves, to keep their churches going. Like Judas, they are stealing the funds entrusted to them for the needy. But they may use their assets generously and humbly, like Mary, offering them freely to Jesus and finding him in the people around them.

The people who joined these studies did so as part of their personal Lent devotions. The insights they drew from the sessions were personal too. They commented that these Bible readings had helped to bring the Gospel stories alive and fresh again. The group had responded wholeheartedly: the sessions never flagged, our discussions were vibrant, quirky and entertaining. Nevertheless, the sessions were informed by the season. The group felt a sense of approaching tragedy. They were particularly aware of evil doers in the texts: Herod, Pilate, Judas and the Pharisees. People were troubled by them and tried to understand them, frankly acknowledging that they recognized aspects of this evil in themselves, and perceiving a need to address it by seeking forgiveness. Yet sorrow was balanced by love: as one person observed, 'There is an outpouring of love in each story.' The group found this love in the person of Jesus. By the end of the series, they thought they had a better understanding of him, of his skill as a teacher, his compassion, his suffering and his determination to fulfil his mission.

Through reading and thinking about the stories together, they felt the Holy Spirit beginning to 'bend' their lives according to Christ. In particular, some said that reading the Bible using the CBS method had helped them understand their own private situations, and to entrust those situations to God. Some people felt that they already had a clearer sense of his plan for their lives. A young woman in the group shared that, in thinking about the passage from John's Gospel, she had found a way forward, as she tried to work out how she was being called to serve the poor in the future. This 'bending' towards Christ was already bearing fruit in the corporate life of the group, in their kindliness to one another, their listening, and their forbearance with each other's small shortcomings. The transforming power of the Gospel was indeed at work in the crypt of St Bride's Church, Hyndland.

Examples of CBS with larger groups

Most of the work that we have described in this book has been with (relatively) small groups, anything from six to 50 or 60 at most. It is quite possible for two reasonably experienced facilitators to work with those sorts of numbers without additional resources. We have very comfortably conducted taster sessions for groups of 50 or so consisting entirely of people who were unfamiliar with the process. In such cases, it is important that the facilitators are well prepared and have worked out beforehand how they will divide up the time available: for example, when to go into small groups, how much time to allow for feedback, how they will organize the seating and ensure that everyone can see the flip chart (or whatever method of recording people's responses is chosen).

Occasionally, we have been asked to conduct studies for much larger groups. Three examples stand out and are worth recording to suggest something of the adaptability of the method and its wider applications. We are sure that it could be used in many other different and creative ways. Two of these ways concern work with school groups. On one occasion in the late 1990s we were invited to conduct a Bible study for Holy Trinity High School, Renfrew, a Catholic secondary school which was concluding a 24-hour fast in aid of SCIAF, the Scottish Catholic International Aid Fund, with a disco and overnight stay at the school. A former member of our CBS group, Hugh Foy, was an RE teacher at the school. He thought that it would be good to start the evening off with a CBS to allow the students to reflect on issues of global justice. We were mildly apprehensive.

On such occasions it is clearly important not only for the facilitators to be well prepared but also to train or prepare others to take part in the facilitation process. How do you engage and hold the attention and interest of a group of about 130 fifth- and sixth-formers who are looking forward to a disco? In this case we were fortunate in having a contact on the staff who was fully acquainted with the process and could recruit and brief his colleagues, who themselves had very impressive skills when it came to dealing with a large group of excited teenagers. The evening started with some 'ice-breakers' in the main assembly hall, which helped the group get settled in and let off a certain amount of steam. At that point, Hugh got the students sitting down on the floor (there were no chairs), introduced the topic for the study and invited John Riches to say something about the process and the role of the Bible in Africa. There followed a dramatic reading by some of the students of the story of Naboth's vineyard from 1 Kings 21. This powerful and violent story of corruption and injustice in high places, read out by a group of fellow students, which was almost certainly quite unknown to the majority, made a deep impact.

We then divided the students up into groups of 12 to 15, each with their own facilitator from among the staff and senior students, who met in different classrooms. We divided the evening into two: first, the close reading of the story with an analysis of its various characters, Ahab, Naboth, Jezebel, Elijah; then the attempt to draw out parallels between the story and present-day society, national and international. After each session the groups returned to the main hall to report back.

The evening undoubtedly worked well. The strange and unfamiliar – and violent – story caught the students' attention. They enjoyed analysing the details of the story and entering into the world of the text. They also enjoyed identifying figures in the contemporary world, from characters in *Coronation Street* to well-known politicians, whose complicity in international and local injustice could be compared with the behaviour of Ahab and Jezebel. There was no sense that they were just waiting for the Bible study to finish so that they could get on with their disco.

On another two occasions we were invited to run Bible studies for a day conference, held in the University of Glasgow, of fifth- and sixth-formers drawn from schools across the West of Scotland. Some 200 to 250 students first gathered in the University Union and then moved around to different locations for various workshops. All of this was organized by SCIAF. On one occasion the theme was 'asylum seekers' and we were asked to conduct a series of Bible studies relating to the theme. We chose Psalm 137, 'By the waters of Babylon', to illustrate the experience and feelings of those in exile. And, because we had to run a series of workshops simultaneously, we fielded a much bigger team of facilitators, drawn from those whom we had trained and who had been working on their own, facilitating discussion groups. This on the whole worked well.

Because of the dispersal of the conference over a large urban campus, there was perhaps less focus and concentration than had been possible in the context of a single school. There were one or two groups where some of the participants seemed not to be fully aware of what the theme of the day was. This meant that the facilitators had to work harder to introduce the topic and to get the readers' attention. But some of the groups worked extremely well. There was a wide variety among the participants, who came from different areas of the city and different faith communities, and included many with little or no religious background at all. Certainly this beautiful, passionate and violent text shocked and fascinated, providing a powerful means for participants to enter imaginatively into the feelings of those who live in exile.

A third opportunity for larger group work was offered by the Scottish Episcopal Church's Provincial Conference. This is an event which has taken place every four or five years and has enabled lay and clerical members of the Church to meet and network, to encourage and inspire each other, nurturing the different initiatives that spring up in a quite dispersed, small but vigorous minority church community. In 2004 we were invited to take part in the organization of the conference, which was to focus on the theme of discerning the gifts and resources available within the Church to carry out its mission. Two of our members, John McLuckie and Stephen Smyth, formed part of the organizing committee and together devised a conference based around an extended study of Mark 6.30–44, the story of the feeding of the five thousand. Throughout the three days of the conference, participants met at regular intervals in small groups to consider what light this story could shed on their experience of discipleship in a Church whose means seemed wholly disproportionate to the tasks they were being called to undertake. Interspersed between these discussions were various presentations, including a rich reflection on the text by Rowan Williams, and an exhibition of various practical initiatives in the life of the Province.

Again it was necessary to make substantial preparation for this kind of extensive work. Two of the staff of the Episcopal Church, Anne Tomlinson and Susan Wiffin (now Macdonald), ran a series of training courses with input from the CBS group to prepare some 60 small-group leaders at the conference for their roles. This not only meant that the conference ran smoothly and that there were a good number of people attending who were well prepared for it. It provided a pool of theological educators and facilitators for the Episcopal Church that has subsequently stood it in good stead and meant that CBS has become a familiar aspect of its small-group work.

Part Two

CONTEXTUAL BIBLE STUDIES FOR ADVENT AND LENT

Using the studies in this book

As we have examined Contextual Bible Study in the earlier chapters of this book, we have heard the stories of many people in a variety of locations who have discovered that the Bible is approachable. A book which often seemed full of strange secrets has been opened up to such people. They have discovered stories from a past which may appear strange and alien, but which nonetheless have something to say about these people's present. In their reading they have explored their thoughts about God and their own lives; their discoveries have been valued and appreciated by others. Readers opening their Bibles in the company of others have discovered new insights and deepened friendships, learning to relate to other people in a more significant way. They have understood the ways of God in their lives differently from before.

We offer the studies that follow in this book in the belief that something fresh and transforming can happen through the meeting of small groups, sometimes for a limited period, such as Lent or Advent, sometimes over a longer time. The studies are based on ones that have already been used in small groups. We hope that those who use them will find in the Bible new ways of understanding the way they should live. This is an invitation to explore the Bible as a gift that is for life.

The Bible studies presented in the following pages always start with the same question: 'What jumps off the page at you?' This is intended to allow the participants to give first reactions to the text, without implying that there will be any right or wrong answers. It encourages the participants simply to read and observe. This is what we mean by 'reading the text', observing closely what is there, registering anything that might be puzzling or suggestive or raising further questions.

The next questions in the study reinforce the idea of reading the text closely. They will often focus on characters in the text; on groups and on the way different people relate and react to one another; the kinds of actions which take place; or the notes of time and place. Sometimes these questions will allow the members of the group to think about what kinds of motivations the characters have for the actions they take, and will allow people to bring forward different interpretations of what is going on. These questions will guide the readers towards particular themes which they will be invited to discuss further later in the study. This is what is referred to as 'reading in front of the text'.

The drawing out of themes will regularly form the basis of the third part of the study, where participants are asked to explore the ways in which their reading of the text might find connections with their past experience or with the issues that they currently face in their lives.

Key

The letters in italic show how the group may be organized for each question. Please note that these are offered as a guide, to be adapted as seems suitable in different circumstances.

3s   work in groups of three
FB feedback in the full group
FG work in the full group

The Gospel readings for Advent

Questions for Advent – Year A

DATE	**Advent One**
TEXT	**Matthew 24.36–44**
THEME	**The coming of the Son of Man**

Question 1   What jumps off the page at you?   *3s, FB*

Question 2   Identify the scenes from everyday life
that Jesus describes in the passage.   *FG*

Question 3   How do you think this passage might
have been heard by the original
audience?   *3s, FB*

Question 4   What might this message mean to
people hearing it today?   *FG*

Question 5   a) How do people usually prepare for
Christmas?

b) How might the message of this passage
of the coming of the Son of Man challenge
or affect how Christians prepare for
Christmas?   *3s, FB*

Question 6   How does our reading of the passage
challenge us this Advent?   *FG*

DATE	**Advent Two**
TEXT	**Matthew 3.1–12**
THEME	**John the Baptist**

Question 1	What jumps off the page at you?	3s, FB
Question 2	Describe what the different characters in the passage are doing.	FG
Question 3	a) What images does John use to proclaim his message?	
	b) What do these images suggest about the Kingdom of Heaven?	FG
Question 4	What do you think John's message means for the Church?	3s, FB
Question 5	How might the Church 'make straight the Way of the Lord' (v. 3)?	3s, FB
Question 6	How does our reading of the passage challenge us this Advent?	FG

DATE	**Advent Three**
TEXT	**Matthew 11.2–11**
THEME	**John the Baptist and Jesus**

Question 1	What jumps off the page at you?	3s, FB
Question 2	Looking carefully at the passage, what can we say about Jesus' attitude towards John?	3s, FB
Question 3	From the text, why does Jesus react as he does to:	
	a) John's disciples?	
	b) the crowd?	FG
Question 4	What does the passage tell us about the 'values' of the Messiah?	FG

Question 5	Where may these values be found in society today?	3s, FB
Question 6	How does our reading of the passage challenge us this Advent?	FG

DATE	**Advent Four**
TEXT	**Matthew 1.18–25**
THEME	**The birth of Jesus – Joseph's dream**

Question 1	What jumps off the page at you?	3s, FB
Question 2	Who are the different characters in the story, and what do they do?	FG
Question 3	What does the passage tell us about Joseph?	FG
Question 4	What might the message 'God with us' (v. 23) have meant, in practical terms, for Joseph and his family?	3s, FB
Question 5	What might the message 'God with us' mean for us today: a) emotionally? b) practically?	3s, FB
Question 6	How will *you* welcome 'God with us'?	3s, FB

Questions for Advent – Year B

DATE	**Advent One**
TEXT	**Mark 13.24–37**
THEME	**Christ's coming**

Question 1	What jumps off the page at you?	3s, FB
Question 2	List the images of warnings and hope/ consolation you see in the passage.	FG

Question 3	What does this passage suggest about Mark's community and its situation?	FG
Question 4	What does this particular passage tell us about Jesus?	3s, FB
Question 5	In the light of this reflection, how might we understand the coming of Christ in our day?	FG
Question 6	What might 'staying awake' mean for you/us this Advent?	3s, FB

DATE	**Advent Two**
TEXT	**Mark 1.1–8**
THEME	**The beginning of Mark's Gospel**

Question 1	What jumps off the page at you?	3s, FB
Question 2	What do we learn from this passage about John the Baptist?	FG
Question 3	What role does John fulfil in this passage?	FG
Question 4	What does this particular passage tell us about Jesus?	3s, FB
Question 5	Where might you recognize the prophetic word being spoken today?	FG
Question 6	How might our reflection help you/us to prepare for a more meaningful celebration of Christ's coming this year?	3s, FB

DATE	**Advent Three**
TEXT	**John 1.6–8, 19–28**
THEME	**John the Baptist's ministry**

| *Question 1* | What jumps off the page at you? | 3s, FB |

Question 2	What does this passage tell us about the kind of expectations the priests and Levites had, and how they responded to John?	*3s, FB*
Question 3	What do you think the Gospel is telling us about John the Baptist, and how does the author present the relationship between John and Jesus?	*FG*
Question 4	What does this particular passage tell us about Jesus?	*3s, FB*
Question 5	Where are the witnesses who testify to Christ today? What expectations does the world have of them?	*FG*
Question 6	How might you/we be challenged or affirmed by our exploration of this passage, as we go into the last two weeks of Advent?	*3s, FB*

DATE	**Advent Four**
TEXT	**Luke 1.26–38**
THEME	**Mary hears news from Gabriel**

Question 1	What jumps off the page at you?	*3s, FB*
Question 2	Name and describe all the relationships you discern within the passage.	*FG*
Question 3	What might these relationships say to us about how God is at work in the world?	*FG*
Question 4	What does this particular passage tell us about Jesus?	*3s, FB*
Question 5	How might God be inviting us or challenging us to carry Christ into today's world?	*3s, FB*
Question 6	What might you/we take away from our shared reading of these Advent reflections?	*FG*

Questions for Advent – Year C

DATE   **Advent One**

TEXT   **Luke 21.25–36 (some lectionaries omit vv. 29–33)**

THEME   **The coming of the Son of Man**

Question 1   What jumps off the page at you?   *3s, FB*

Question 2   List all the 'end-times' or 'apocalyptic' language and images you find in the passage. *FG*

Question 3   How do you feel about this kind of language and imagery?   *3s, FB*

Question 4   What does Jesus say about how his disciples should prepare 'to stand before the Son of Man' (v. 36)?   *FG*

Question 5   In our world today, where does Jesus' message especially need to be heard and heeded?   *3s, FB*

Question 6   As we begin Advent, what will you/we take away from our reflections on this Gospel passage?   *3s, FB*

DATE   **Advent Two**

TEXT   **Luke 3.1–6**

THEME   **John prepares the way of Christ**

Question 1   What jumps off the page at you?   *3s, FB*

Question 2   How would you describe the different styles of writing employed in this passage? *FG*

Question 3   Why do you think Luke chooses to bring together two very different styles of writing like this?   *FG*

Question 4	In verses 4–6, what is Luke trying to tell us about how to 'prepare the way of the Lord'?	3s, FG
Question 5	In our world today, which valleys need to be filled, or mountains and hills made low?	3s, FB
Question 6	Is there any idea/image/feeling from our reflections on this Gospel passage that you find particularly affirming or challenging?	3s, FB

DATE	**Advent Three**
TEXT	**Luke 3.7–18 (some lectionaries omit vv. 7–9)**
THEME	**John the Baptist teaches the crowd**

Question 1	What jumps off the page at you?	3s, FB
Question 2	List all the verbs or 'doing words' you find in the passage.	FG
Question 3	What effect do you think John's teaching would have had upon his hearers?	FG
Question 4	If today you (individual or group) were to ask John, 'What then should we do?', what do you think his challenge to you would be?	3s, FB
Question 5	How do you feel about the image of the Messiah given in verses 15–17?	3s, FB
Question 6	How might this passage help us to shape our celebration of Christmas?	FG

DATE   **Advent Four**
TEXT   **Luke 1.39–44 (some lectionaries also**
                include vv. 45–55)
THEME   **Mary visits Elizabeth**

Question 1   What jumps off the page at you?   *3s, FB*
Question 2   What feelings or emotions might we
                attribute to the characters mentioned in
                the passage?   *FG*
Question 3   What feeling or emotion are you left
                with from our reading of this passage?   *3s, FB*
Question 4   What is Elizabeth saying to us about the
                Son of Mary?   *FG*
Question 5   How might you/we share more
                meaningfully with others the blessings
                we receive in the Son of Mary?   *3s, FB*
Question 6   Is there any particular blessing or gift
                that you have received through your
                experience of sharing the scriptures
                with this group?   *3s, FB*

The Gospel readings for Lent

Questions for Lent – Year A

DATE   **Lent One**
TEXT   **Matthew 4.1–11**
THEME   **Jesus is tempted in the wilderness**

Question 1	What jumps off the page at you?	*3s, FB*
Question 2	Name the choices that the Tempter offers Jesus. How does Jesus respond to these choices?	*FG*
Question 3	What influenced Jesus in making these decisions?	*FG*
Question 4	Why does the Gospel writer include this episode at the start of Jesus' ministry?	*3s, FB*
Question 5	What kind of choices do you face as you try to live out your faith today?	*3s, FB*
Question 6	Where in this passage might you find support?	*FG*

DATE   **Lent Two**
TEXT   **John 3.1–17**
THEME   **Nicodemus visits Jesus at night**

Question 1	What jumps off the page at you?	*3s, FB*
Question 2	What terms are used to express the contrast between old and new life in this passage?	*FG*

Question 3	From the passage, what does it mean for God to love the world?	FG
Question 4	a) Why is it that 'the world' needs to be saved?	
	b) What does the passage tell us about God's action in saving the world?	3s, FB
Question 5	How do we see the role of our congregation/group in God's loving action towards the world?	3s, FB
Question 6	What challenges does this present to us?	FG

DATE	**Lent Two (alternative lectionary reading)**
TEXT	**Matthew 17.1–9**
THEME	**The Transfiguration**

Question 1	What jumps off the page at you?	3s, FB
Question 2	Identify the different small scenes that make up this story.	FG
Question 3	Select one or two key moments and examine them more closely, from the point of view of a) Jesus	
	b) the disciples	3s, FB
Question 4	Why do you think Jesus says, 'Tell no one about the vision until after the Son of Man has been raised from the dead' (v. 9)?	FG
Question 5	In the light of the disciples' difficulties, what role does misunderstanding play in discipleship?	3s, FB
Question 6	Given Jesus' command to silence, are there any aspects of Christian experience and belief where we need to exercise restraint, when talking about them?	3s, FB

DATE	**Lent Three**
TEXT	**John 4.5–42**
THEME	**Jesus and the Samaritan woman at the well**

Question 1	What jumps off the page at you?	*3s, FB*
Question 2	What does the passage say about the place of the woman in her community?	*FG*
Question 3	How does Jesus reach out to her?	*FG*
Question 4	In what ways can you identify with the woman and her experience of meeting Jesus?	*3s, FB*
Question 5	How does the image of 'living water' help you to make sense of this experience?	*3s, FB*
Question 6	Where are the unexpected places in which we might find wells of living water today?	*FG*

DATE	**Lent Four**
TEXT	**John 9.1–41**
THEME	**Jesus heals the man born blind**

A dramatic reading and discussion: the facilitators organize the group into readers and the passage into small scenes. Each small scene in the passage is acted out. Give each scene 2–3 minutes.

Question 1	Is there anything that struck you?	*FG*
Question 2	How did it feel to act the part of the blind man? A Pharisee? The man's neighbours? His parents? Did you feel changed at all as the story went on?	*3s, FB*
Question 3	What times have there been in your experience, when new life/new sight has seemed to come into your church/group	

	and there have been negative reactions to it?	3s, FB
Question 4	Take roles and act out one of these contemporary contexts and its consequences.	FG
Question 5	Discuss how you think about such situations now, in the light of what you have read and heard. How do you feel? How might you deal with them in the future?	FG

DATE	**Lent Five**
TEXT	**John 11.1–45**
THEME	**The death and raising of Lazarus**

This is the longest passage in our series of studies. As you read the passage, please pay particular attention to the experiences of Mary and Martha, the sisters of Lazarus.

Question 1	What jumps off the page at you?	3s, FB
Question 2	Describe the reactions and emotions of Mary and Martha. In what ways are they similar, in what ways different?	FG
Question 3	Compare the reactions and emotions of Mary and Martha in this passage with those of other individuals and groups.	3s, FB
Question 4	What does the passage teach us about Jesus?	FG
Question 5	In what ways does this story resonate with your experience in your church/ community today?	3s, FB
Question 6	Share with the group any new insight you have received from your sharing of this passage.	FG

Questions for Lent – Year B

DATE   **Lent One**
TEXT   **Mark 1.9–15**
THEME   **The baptism and temptation of Jesus**

Question 1   What jumps off the page at you?   *3s, FB*

Question 2   List all the different actions that are
mentioned in the passage. Who does what?   *FG*

Question 3   This is the first time we see Jesus in Mark's
Gospel. What does *this passage* tell you
about what the rest of the book will be
about?   *3s, FB*

Question 4   From the passage, what do you understand
by 'Kingdom of God' and 'preaching Good
News' (vv. 14–15)? What obstacles were
there to proclaiming the Good News at
the time Jesus began his ministry?   *3s, FB*

Question 5   How should we interpret 'Kingdom of God'
and 'Good News' in our own situation?   *FG*

Question 6   What hinders us in our proclamation of
good news? How might we overcome this?   *3s, FB*

DATE   **Lent Two**
TEXT   **Mark 8.31–38**
THEME   **Tough Teaching**

Question 1   What jumps off the page at you?   *3s, FB*

Question 2   What demands do the main characters
make of each other in the text?   *FG*

Question 3   How do you feel about the way that
Jesus speaks to Peter in verse 33?   *3s, FB*

Question 4	a) What might it mean, for a generation to be 'adulterous and sinful' (v. 38)?
	b) How far do you think that this is a fair description of present generations? *3s, FB*
Question 5	What is the cross that you/your group needs to take up? *3s, FB*
Question 6	Where might Jesus be asking you to carry the cross? *3s, FB*

DATE   **Lent Two (alternative lectionary reading)**
TEXT   **Mark 9.2–10**
THEME   **The Transfiguration**

Question 1	What jumps off the page at you? *3s, FB*
Question 2	Paying close attention to the text, identify what the three disciples witnessed during this incident. *FG*
Question 3	a) What do you think they understood at the time?
	b) What do you think they came to understand later? *3s, FB*
Question 4	Where might this passage resonate most with Jesus' followers and the issues they face in the world today? *FG*
Question 5	Are there important things that you have understood in one way at a particular point in your life, and have later come to understand differently? What new insights caused this change of mind? *3s, FB*
Question 6	Are there issues in your own life, or in the life of your congregation/group, which need to be 'transfigured'? *3s, FB*

DATE	**Lent Three**
TEXT	**John 2.13–25 (some lectionaries finish at v. 22)**
THEME	**The incident in the Temple**

Question 1 What jumps off the page at you?   *3s, FB*

Question 2 Paying close attention to the text, identify what Jesus' disciples witnessed during this incident.   *FG*

Question 3 a) What do you think they understood at the time?
b) What do you think they came to understand later?   *3s, FB*

Question 4 a) What are the main tensions that you can identify in this passage?
b) Which of these issues are still alive today?   *FG*

Question 5 What kind of response to the tensions you have identified is being asked for by disciples today?   *3s, FB*

Question 6 In concrete terms, what might your understanding of what is being asked of disciples mean in your own local situation?   *FG*

DATE	**Lent Four**
TEXT	**John 3.14–21**
THEME	**God's Son in the world**

Question 1 What jumps off the page at you?   *3s, FB*

Question 2 In this passage, what do you identify as being
a) signs of light?
b) signs of darkness?   *FG*

105

Question 3   What do you think the Gospel writer
             wants the reader to understand about
             Jesus and his teaching?   *3s, FB*

Question 4   From the passage, what distinguishes those
             who remain in darkness from those who
             come to the light? Do these distinctions
             resonate with your own experience?   *3s, FB*

Question 5   How might the teaching we find in this
             passage be received today by
             a) those within the Church community?
             b) those who are not part of the Church
                community?   *FG*

Question 6   From your experience, what situations of
             light and dark do you know of that this
             passage might speak to?   *3s, FB*

DATE   **Lent Five**
TEXT   **John 12.20–33 (some lectionaries end at v. 30)**
THEME   **The Son of Man will be glorified**

Question 1   What jumps off the page at you?   *3s, FB*
Question 2   Name the images and ideas in this passage
             that have to do with life and death.   *FG*
Question 3   From this passage, what do you think
             Jesus is saying
             a) about his own life?
             b) about the lives of those who hear
                his words?   *3s, FB*
Question 4   How does the passage explore the
             relationship between glory and suffering?   *3s, FB*
Question 5   What resonance does this have in
             contemporary society, or in the experience
             of your congregation/group?   *FG*

Question 6   In what ways might your discussion of suffering and glory help you as a group preparing to turn towards the Easter story of the death and resurrection of Jesus?   *FG*

Questions for Lent – Year C

DATE   **Lent One**
TEXT   **Luke 4.1–13**
THEME   **Jesus encounters the devil: 'I'll be back!'**

Question 1   What jumps off the page at you?   *3s, FB*
Question 2   List all the places that are mentioned. In the context of the passage, what do you think these places represent?   *FG*
Question 3   What do you think the phrase 'until an opportune time' (v. 13) means? In what different ways might you interpret this?   *3s, FB*
Question 4   What does the passage tell us about the places where God is active?   *FG*
Question 5   In your experience, are there unexpected places where God is active?   *3s, FB*
Question 6   In what sense is the present an 'opportune time' for your group/community?   *FG*

DATE   **Lent Two**
TEXT   **Luke 13.31–35***
THEME   **Are we nearly there yet?**

---

* Luke 9.28–36 'The Transfiguration' is an alternative lectionary reading. For suggested questions, see 'The Transfiguration' Year B Lent Two.

Question 1	What jumps off the page at you?	*3s, FB*
Question 2	List all the references to time that you can find in the passage. What does the passage show about the time scale that Jesus has for his ministry?	*FG*
Question 3	What insights does this passage give about the character of Jesus?	*FG*
Question 4	Can you think of times when a heavy price has been paid for doing what is right? You may think about your own personal experience, that of your group/ community, or the experience of other people who currently face difficult choices.	*3s, FB*
Question 5	Are there signs of healing/hope in the difficult situations you have discussed? If so, what can be done to encourage these?	*FG*
Question 6	Reread the passage. Does the character of Jesus as you have discussed it in this study give us insight into the way that we respond to difficult situations? What challenges do we receive from the example of Jesus for our current circumstances?	*3s, FB*

DATE	**Lent Three**
TEXT	**Luke 13.1–9**
THEME	**Big questions and hard answers**

Question 1	What jumps off the page at you?	*3s, FB*
Question 2	a) Focusing on verses 1–5, identify all the groups and characters mentioned directly in this passage.	

b) Focusing on verses 6–9, list all the different stages of action/moments in the parable. *FG*

Question 3 What political and religious questions are raised by the events described in verses 1–5? *FG*

Question 4 Looking closely at the text, why do you think Jesus chose to use this parable in response to the current news stories told to him in verses 1–5? *3s, FB*

Question 5 What are the big stories making today's headlines that might lead people to ask 'big questions'? What are the issues that are raised for you by these stories? *3s, FB*

Question 6 Does this passage address any issues faced by you as an individual/group/community? What challenges might the parable present to the issue(s) you have identified? *FG*

DATE	**Lent Four**
TEXT	**Luke 15.1–3, 11–32**
THEME	**A father and two sons**

Question 1 What jumps off the page at you? *3s, FB*

Question 2 Describe the actions and attitudes of the father and his two sons. Identify all the examples of 'good behaviour' and 'bad behaviour' you can find in this passage. *FG*

Question 3 Imagine yourself as the father in this story. Retell the story as you find it in Luke's Gospel, from the father's point of view. *FG*

Question 4   Discuss what this passage tells us about
ONE of the following:
a) the nature of God
b) our relationship with God
c) our relationships with one another   *3s, FB*

The following questions are intended to be personal. You will be invited to share some of your thoughts in the small group. One or two people may also wish to share with the full group afterwards. Please only share what you are comfortable offering in a group. Please remember to respect the confidentiality of what is shared in the group.

Question 5   a) Think of an occasion when, like the two sons,
you were challenged to have a change of heart.
b) Think of an occasion when, like the
father, you were challenged to be forgiving
and to welcome someone back.   *3s, FB*

Question 6   Do the retelling of this familiar parable and
the sharing of stories from your context give
new insights into how you might address a
current situation in your community/group/
wider society? Is there something that you
feel in the light of this study that you are
being asked to do?   *3s, FB*

DATE   **Lent Five**
TEXT   **John 12.1–8**
THEME   **Anointing at Bethany**

Question 1   What jumps off the page at you?   *3s, FB*
Question 2   List all the characters and their

	relationships in this passage.	*FG*
Question 3	Paying close attention to the text, take one of these characters and explore the incident through his or her eyes.	*3s, FB*
Question 4	What are the big themes addressed in this passage?	*FG*
Question 5	Choose ONE of these big themes and explore it. How does that theme resonate with issues that are faced in your own life or in wider society? What challenges does the passage present to you as individuals or to our society?	*3s, FB*
Question 6	This is the last in our series of studies. Think over your experience of these sessions. Share with the group a memorable conversation that you have had in the studies, or an important insight that you carry forward from these studies.	*FG*

Notes

1 E. Anum, 'Towards Intercultural Contextual Bible Study: A review of the adoption of Contextual Bible Study (from South Africa) in the West of Scotland', *International Review of Mission*, 91/361 (2002), p. 225.

2 Anum, 'Towards Intercultural Contextual Bible Study', p. 229.

3 C. Brown, *Religion and Society in Scotland since 1707* (Edinburgh: Edinburgh University Press, 1997), p. 158.

4 G. West, 'Contextuality', in J. F. A. Sawyer (ed.), *The Blackwell Companion to the Bible and Culture* (Oxford: Blackwell, 2006), p. 401.

5 Anum, 'Towards Intercultural Contextual Bible Study', p. 229.

6 L. Lawrence, *The Word in Place: Reading the New Testament in contemporary contexts* (London: SPCK, 2009); A. Peden, 'Contextual Bible Study at Cornton Vale Women's Prison, Stirling', *The Expository Times*, 117:1 (2005).

7 Peden, 'Contextual Bible Study', p. 15.

8 Peden, 'Contextual Bible Study', p. 15.

9 'Worship Resources', *The Expository Times*, 117:9 (2006), pp. 373–7; 'Worship Resources', *The Expository Times*, 118:2 (2006), pp. 83–4.

10 H. de Wit et al. (eds), *Through the Eyes of Another: Intercultural readings of the Bible* (Amsterdam: Institute of Mennonite Studies, 2004).

11 J. Riches, 'Ephesians', in D. Patte (ed.), *Global Bible Commentary* (Nashville: Abingdon, 2004).

12 See for instance Ernesto Cardinale, *The Gospel in Solentiname*.

13 Lawrence, *The Word in Place*, pp. 60–73.